Formative Assessment
in the New Balanced Literacy Classroom

Margaret Mary Policastro

Becky McTague

Diane Mazeski

Maupin House *by*
capstone
professional

Formative Assessment in the New Balanced Literacy Classroom
By Margaret Mary Policastro, Becky McTague, and Diane
Mazeski

Cover Design: Richard Parker
Book Design: Jodi Pedersen

Photo Credits:
Front cover: Shutterstock
Back cover: Margaret Mary Policastro by Bob Coscarelli, Becky
McTague by Rachael McTague, and Diane Mazeski by Sandy
Smolinski

Library of Congress Cataloging-in-Publication Data
Cataloging-in-publication information is on file with the
Library of Congress.

978-1-4966-0295-4 (pbk.)
978-1-4966-0296-1 (eBook PDF)
978-1-4966-0297-8 (eBook)

Maupin House publishes professional resources for K–12 educators. Contact us for tailored, in-school training or to schedule
an author for a workshop or conference. Visit www.maupin-
house.com for free lesson plan downloads.

Maupin House Publishing, Inc. by Capstone Professional
1710 Roe Crest Drive
North Mankato, MN 56003

www.maupinhouse.com
888-262-6135
info@maupinhouse.com

Dedication

We are both privileged and fortunate to work side by side with teachers and school leaders in both urban and suburban schools. We dedicate this book to all teachers and school leaders who are striving to merge instruction and assessment into a formative assessment community. We understand what dedication this takes from both the school leaders to create such a culture and the teachers to employ pedagogy that is at times difficult.

We are honored to work with teachers in the Chicago Public Schools and the Archdiocese of Chicago. Therefore, we specifically dedicate this book to the following schools where the school leaders and teachers go many extra miles to move children forward in their learning: Perkins Bass Elementary School, Chicago, Illinois; Orville T. Bright Elementary School, Chicago, Illinois; Christ the King School, Chicago, Illinois; John C. Dore Elementary School, Chicago, Illinois; Metcalfe Community Academy, Chicago, Illinois; and Our Lady of the Wayside School, Arlington Heights, Illinois. These teachers have made a dedicated commitment to the moment-by-moment decision-making involved in formative assessment. Their hard work is put forth daily and we appreciate and celebrate that work. These schools represent school change and commitment to best practices at the highest level.

Acknowledgments

The idea for this book all started with Dr. Dianne Gardner from Illinois State University and the Illinois Board of Higher Education (IBHE). Dianne serves as an evaluator for our IBHE grant. Her passion and dedication for formative assessment is contagious and thus propelled us forward to write this book. We also want to acknowledge the Illinois Board of Higher Education for the funding for our work in the schools, and we'd specifically like to acknowledge Rich Jachino. Our work in the schools is joyful as we work alongside both school leaders and teachers.

A special acknowledgment goes to Karen Soll, Managing Editor at Capstone Professional. Karen has a keen style for providing formative feedback. She clearly understands the process of formative feedback, which includes moving the learner forward. From the initial proposal stages to this manuscript, she has been enormously influential in her feedback and suggestions.

We want to acknowledge Dr. Thomas Philion, Dean of the College of Education at Roosevelt University, who supports all of our efforts both in the clinic and with the grant. Thanks to the Office of Community Engagement at Roosevelt University for support in our grant work. We'd especially like to thank Dr. Teryl Rosch and Jeanne Barnas. A special thanks to John MacDougall for assisting with the photographs and getting them just right. These people work behind the scenes so we can bring formative assessment into the new balanced literacy schools. We want to acknowledge the Roosevelt University literacy coaches that work side by side with the school leaders and coaches: Melissa Marquino Peterson and Marlene Levin. We also want to recognize our outside evaluators from Loyola University, Dr. Leanne Kallemeyn, Dr. Diane Morrison, and Jana Grabarek, who have worked with us from the initial stages of the grant until today.

Our work and this book would not have happened without our IBHE grant partner schools who have welcomed us daily into their community of learners. We would like to acknowledge the following principals and administrators from the Archdiocese of Chicago Catholic Schools and the Chicago Public Schools (CPS) who so welcomed us into their community: Alicia Lewis and Dr. Pam Strauther-Sanders from Orville T. Bright Elementary School in Chicago, Illinois; Stephen Fabiyi and Miyoshi Brown from Metcalfe Community Academy in Chicago, Illinois; Dr. AnnMarie Riordan from Christ the King School in Chicago, Illinois; Dr. Elizabeth Alvarez and Sean McNichols from John C. Dore Elementary School in Chicago, Illinois; David Wood and Pat Gatewood from Our Lady of the Wayside School in Arlington Heights, Illinois; Carolyn Jones from Perkins Bass Elementary School in Chicago, Illinois; and Dr. Steven Meyers, Roosevelt University Professor of Psychology for his unending guidance on self-monitoring practices.

We also want to acknowledge Sharon Roth and Lara Hebert from the National Center for Literacy Education (NCLE). Their unending support of our work has been invaluable. The feedback that they provide has allowed us to understand capacity building and the important connections to school-wide formative assessment systems.

There are many Roosevelt University graduate students who participated in our clinical practicum, which is the summer reading clinic. During the summer of 2014, we piloted our formative assessment model in their classrooms, so we would be ready to take the model out into our partner schools in the fall. We are most grateful for their willingness to stand by us and take a risk with us. These students include LaWanda Jones, Beth Cha, Kerry Campbell, Keri Klein, Dominique Watson, and Parul Patel. We also want to give a hearty acknowledgment to the clinic volunteers, Ellen Pape, Shannon Hart, Amy Carroll, and Daisy Rakipi, who came on a daily basis to assist in all aspects of the important work. We want to thank Jorie Sutton, our graduate assistant, and Valerie Mercurio, our student worker in the Office of Community Engagement, who have been on call for us since August 2014, collecting resources, checking our citations, and doing much more.

Finally, we thank our families, who have supported all of our work over many years and especially while writing this book.

Formative Assessment in the New Balanced Literacy Classroom

Table of Contents

Foreword

"We understand that the formative assessment process of teaching is hard and complex, perhaps the most rigorous type of pedagogy."

— Policastro, McTague, and Mazeski

We have all heard the mantra "assessment informs instruction," or more strongly stated, "assessment *drives* instruction." In an era of increasing accountability, never has so much attention been focused on the tools and techniques of assessment. Unfortunately much of that attention is often focused on externally mandated summative assessments that, at best, can be used to inform thinking about programs, but do very little to guide our daily thinking about individuals. And when we do focus on individuals, we frequently use quick and easy measures of quantifiable "indicators" that show progress in discrete skills but fall short of capturing the complexities of proficient readers and writers.

Assessment, like instruction, needs to be guided by purpose. As classroom teachers make decisions about assessment, they focus on three key questions: What do I need to know? Why do I need to know it? And what is the best way to find it out? Those questions lead teachers to a need for a different vision of assessment. In *Formative Assessment in the New Balanced Literacy Classroom*, Margaret Mary Policastro, Becky McTague, and Diane Mazeski create that different vision.

Their vision starts with acknowledging the important role of formative assessment. The boundary between instruction and assessment is removed. As the authors observe, the more assessment and instruction are seen as integrated entities, the more the teacher sees *each point of instruction* as an opportunity for collecting *formative data on each student's process of learning*.

This deliberate decision-making is a perfect example of how balanced literacy instruction merges with formative assessment, causing a perfect confluence of differentiated pedagogy. Understanding how children learn best and what instructional practices influence reading and writing must be considered as a basis for schoolwide transformational change.

Virtually every minute in a classroom produces data that can inform our thinking about what to do next with our learners, but large periods of the school day often go untapped. We try to capture what transpires intuitively in our hearts and heads; however, systematic collection, analysis, and use of data during these times are rare. Policastro, McTague, and Mazeski build on their work on the new balanced literacy model by highlighting how formative assessments can be integrated in four key classroom components that are often overlooked as rich sources of data: the read-aloud, guiding language into reading, language and literacy centers, and independent reading and writing. They provide useful tools to guide individual teachers to more effectively use formative assessment—especially in new ways—in their classrooms. The authors' techniques allow for the formative collection of data, a means to provide formative feedback to the student, and ways to encourage formative self-monitoring by the student.

If as everyone says "assessment drives instruction," then the two should operate in tandem. That is seen in the best forms of formative assessment—especially those tools and techniques that allow us to capture rich information from daily classroom routines. In *Formative Assessment in the New Balanced Literacy Classroom*, Policastro, McTague, and Mazeski provide a path toward a more purposeful way of operating in today's classrooms.

— Michael P. Ford
Professor of Reading Education
The University of Wisconsin Oshkosh

Chapter One: Introduction to Formative Assessment and Balanced Literacy

Every summer we run a balanced literacy clinical practicum for five weeks known as the Roosevelt University Summer Reading Clinic. This is where the graduate students complete their clinical practicum in language and literacy to become reading specialists. Over the past 27 summers, we have learned that every minute of instruction and teaching is actually a keen way to assess children. It is in the act of teaching itself that the formative process unfolds. Moreover, keeping track of and documenting the formation of the literacy learning is important. For example, we document students' interests and attitude toward reading and writing and monitor their reading levels, comprehension, listening skills, reader responses, writing, and much more over a five-week period. Our teachers come "clipboard ready" and begin the processes of gathering information about each student and assisting each child in learning how to self-monitor his or her own learning as well. Moreover, we make certain to provide daily feedback to the children and parents. It is this information that begins the formative decision-making process by the teacher.

In addition to our summer work, we spend the academic year working in large urban and suburban public and private schools where we have observed notions and ideas about assessment in schools. What we notice most often is that assessment is commonly viewed as an activity that is perceived as independent of teaching and instruction. The pattern often goes "teach then test, teach then test." We should clarify here, however, that a "test" and formative "assessment" are quite different. We think of a test as a summative assessment tool that a teacher uses to measure the quality or performance of a student. Tests are often given at the end of a unit or lesson, and formats may include question and answer, multiple choice, and fill in the blank. Students typically receive a score from a summative assessment. Within schools, summative assessments are viewed as "high stakes" and are generally perceived as having consequences, such as students not getting a diploma or being able to move to the next grade, teachers being evaluated on their teaching performance by how well their students do on such assessments, or the future of the school being in jeopardy—even school closure. Most often, there is in the community a school-wide capacity assessment building that focuses on "getting test ready" for the summative assessments and on results. For example, some schools have motivational posters placed throughout the school encouraging students to do well on the summative assessments.

Formative assessment is an important dimension to the preparation for summative assessments (tests). This is especially important now as teacher evaluation includes a percentage based on how well the students perform on summative assessments, which include the new Partnership for Assessment of Readiness for College and Careers (PARCC) and Smarter Balanced tests. The percentage of teacher evaluation that is tied to student performance varies by state and district. In one large urban district, around 30 percent of the teacher's evaluation is based on how well students perform on summative assessments. Indeed, it is in the teachers' best interest to guide the students and prepare them to be successful on these summative assessments. It is critical, however, that teachers understand the impact that formative assessment can have on student performance on summative assessments. For example, Shanahan (2014) specifically states "Prepare students to excel on these tests not by focusing instruction on question types but by making students sophisticated and powerful readers." We believe that inherent within balanced literacy is the goal of developing "sophisticated and powerful readers." Shanahan encourages five steps in preparing students for the summative tests. We have added to these steps by explaining how each can be integrated into balanced literacy instruction with examples of formative assessment.

Balanced Literacy, Formative Assessment, and Shanahan's Five Steps for Test Success

Shanahan's Five Steps	Formative Assessment: Balanced Literacy
1. Have students read extensively within instruction.	During guided reading and independent reading, students read silently for different purposes as the teacher constantly observes, **monitors their comprehension** with exit slips (see page 76), and provides feedback when necessary.
2. Have students read increasing amounts of text without guidance or support.	During guided reading and independent reading, students are reading text to build stamina by reading longer selections of text. The **teacher elicits evidence of student learning through self-monitoring** techniques, including exit slips (see page 76).
3. Make sure the texts are rich in content and sufficiently challenging.	Read-aloud selections are both complex and difficult. The teacher monitors student learning with students responding on whiteboards. After the read-aloud, students self-monitor with exit slips, and the **teacher provides feedback to assist in comprehension.**
4. Have students explain their answers and provide text evidence supporting their claims.	During the read-aloud, the teacher asks questions that require students to use whiteboards to explain answers and provide evidence from text. Teacher monitors responses and **provides feedback where needed.**
5. Engage students in writing about text, not just in replying to multiple-choice questions.	Independent writing has built-in purposes of writing both text summaries and syntheses. **Teacher confers with students and provides feedback.**

Charlotte Danielson's *Framework for Teaching Evaluation Instrument,* a widely used tool for teacher evaluation, covers four domains of teaching responsibility. The domains include Planning and Preparation, Classroom Environment, Instruction, and Professional Responsibilities. This tool specifically addresses formative assessment in domains 1 and 3. For example, Danielson explains that to be at the "Distinguished Level" of teacher performance, "Assessment is fully integrated into instruction through extensive use of formative assessment." This teacher evaluation tool explicitly outlines formative assessment as an important responsibility for the teacher. We think that this framework for teaching is in perfect alignment with the new balanced literacy model and formative assessment. Formatively assessing students engaged in the tenets of balanced literacy (read-alouds, guided reading, centers, and independent reading and writing) provides the pedagogy and teacher decision-making for formative assessment to be fully integrated into instruction.

During a recent visit to a first-grade class, a teacher conveyed that her day is spent doing district-wide assessments and that she wished she had time to teach. The teacher informed us that after she completes the testing, there are only 15 minutes left to teach in her literacy block. This teacher was also concerned that she does not have time to use the data collected in the district assessments to inform her teaching. One of the tests she had to administer was a weekly list of words to each child. This list of words was given in isolation and students were tested on reading each word correctly. This form of assessment is summative in nature. The primary difference between formative and summative assessments is that summative typically is a measure of the level of success at the end of a unit. Formative assessment is ongoing throughout the entire unit. We understand the importance of summative assessments especially as we prepare students to be successful on the new Common Core State Standards (CCSS) assessments and national assessments. However, to aid summative assessments, we want to expand the notion of formative assessment to assessing the process of the formation of knowledge. The development of literacy, knowledge, and skills is a complex process with different ways in which it forms and develops for each child. It is this forming of knowledge that is at the heart of formative assessment. We want to document the learning moments, especially when they indicate a new base of knowledge or skill. More importantly, we want students and teachers to document the learning when the learning process is interrupted and the understanding of the knowledge becomes fuzzy or confusing for a learner—leaving a gap in the process of learning.

Our intention is to provide students with "real-time" formative feedback so they can move forward in their learning. Wiggins (2012) describes "timely feedback" as being provided to the students when the information is still fresh in their minds. He describes "untimely feedback" as information given to students days, weeks, or even months after the performance. This type of feedback is not effective if the student has moved on to new and different tasks to perform, leaving less motivation to go back and practice what was taught in the past. Moreover, having students become metacognitive or self-aware of these processes as they are happening is critical to formative assessment. As Afflerbach (2014) states "reading instruction is intended to help students become successful, independent readers. At the heart of independence is the ability to self-assess, and with our careful teaching, we want to foster success as students initiate, work through, and complete reading tasks."

The purpose of this book is to assist teachers and school leaders in the development of school-wide formative assessment practices. More specifically, we want to provide a step-by-step plan for classroom teachers to implement formative assessment. This will involve the merging of teaching and assessment so that the decisions and reflections teachers make are a continuous, or formative, process. We understand that the formative assessment process of teaching is hard and complex, perhaps the most rigorous type of pedagogy. What makes this teaching complex is that instruction and assessment are woven together. Further, as instruction and assessments are carried out, the teacher is making plans and reflecting on teaching to ensure progress and learning. Students are receiving feedback from the teacher in real time and are able to self-monitor their learning progress, but it can be tricky for the teacher to juggle this. If done well, however, this continuous process is actually a means to the summative assessments. If teachers are using formative assessments to ready students for summative knowledge and skills, then there is a continuous flow of differentiated decision-making for each child.

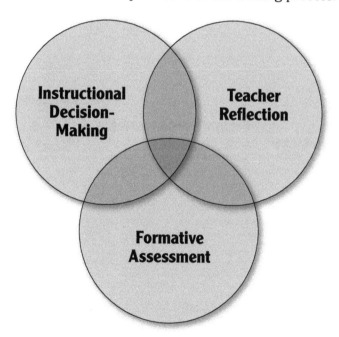

> Today we are having the museum. This week was fun I liked. the mini mystery's And the thing on R.L. Stine
>
> Matt,
> I'm glad that you enjoyed the mini mystery. You did a great job reading.
> Now that you know how R.L. Stine writes you can develop your own mini mystery.

For example, in the student writing sample above, the teacher provided just the right formative feedback to move the student forward in his writing. This feedback gives the student the exact next steps to take in the writing process.

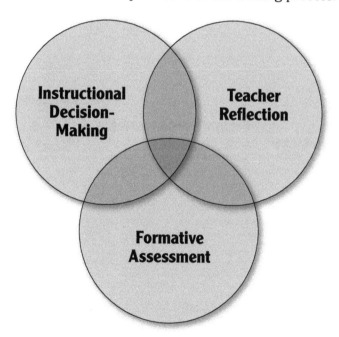

Instructional Decision-Making

Teacher Reflection

Formative Assessment

The figure above shows the overlapping nature and convergence of the processes going on within formative assessment. Another example of weaving instruction and assessment happens during the daily read-aloud when a teacher's observations of students' responses to questions and the text are documented. We have seen many instances in which the teacher will ask questions during a read-aloud and record student responses.

- Do you think about your instruction as assessment?

- Do you think about how instruction and assessment are connected?

- Do you think about how the formation of knowledge and skills unfolds as you teach?

- Do you think about assessment as an ongoing process within instruction?

- How does the balanced literacy model capture and represent formative assessment?

The New Balanced Literacy and Formative Assessment Model

In our book *The New Balanced Literacy School: Implementing Common Core* (Policastro & McTague, 2015), we discuss balanced literacy and how it is now reconceptualized based on the instructional shifts necessary for success with the Common Core State Standards (CCSS).

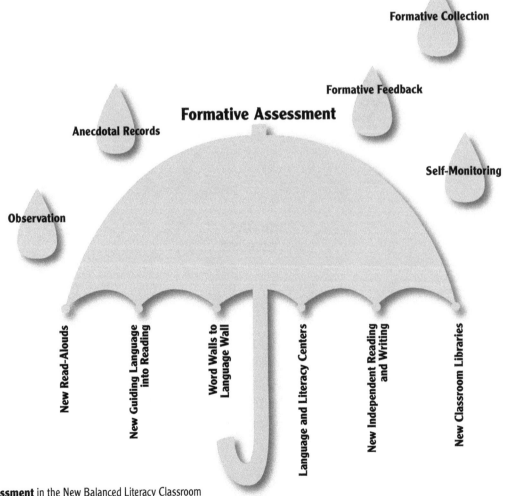

Our overall intention is to weave together—through ongoing and systematic school-wide capacity building—the new balanced literacy model and formative assessments, along with the influence of Common Core. Capacity building (NCLE 2013) is described as the conditions and practices that support effective collaboration and impact student learning. Implied in this quest to build capacity within schools is the notion that the teacher becomes a learner as well, placing learning at the heart of all reform efforts. This goes beyond students and includes the system as a whole and those who work within it (O'Day, J., Goertz, M.E. & Floden, R.E., 1995).

Six Domains of Capacity Building

1. Deprivatizing Practices
2. Enacting Shared Agreement
3. Creating Collaborative Cultures
4. Maintaining an Inquiry Stance
5. Using Evidence Effectively
6. Supporting Collaboration Systemically

To learn more about these domains, visit the website for the National Center for Literacy Education (NCLE).

"Formative assessment is the lived, daily embodiment of a teacher's desire to refine practice based on keener understanding of current levels of student performance, undergirded by the teacher's knowledge of possible paths of student development within the discipline and of pedagogies that support such development" (NCTE, 2013). Balanced literacy is a philosophical approach whereby the teacher makes thoughtful choices about the best way for students to become successful readers and writers (Spiegel, 1998). This deliberate decision-making by the teacher forms the basis for daily instruction and is guided by formative assessment. This instruction includes a daily literacy routine of read-alouds, guided reading, language walls, language and literacy centers, and independent reading and writing. The CCSS takes the position that the "standards are the learning goals for what students should know and be able to do at each grade level. Educational standards help teachers ensure their students have the skills and knowledge they need to be successful while also helping parents understand what is expected of their children" (2014). That is, the Common Core "does not dictate how teachers should teach. Instead schools and teachers will decide how best to help students reach the standards" (2014). An essential component that must be aligned to Common Core instruction is the implementation of formative assessment. In the new balanced literacy school, there is a collaborative effort whereby student learning is documented by formative assessment practices. These practices are shared and decisions are made about student learning in a collaborative manner within grade-level teams. Phillips and Wong (2010) say that states must be sure their standards are coherent, are aligned to assessments, and use formative assessments to determine proficiency.

History of Formative Assessment and Balanced Literacy

Guiding Questions:
- What is the history and definition of formative assessment?
- What is the history and definition of balanced literacy?

Formative assessment is not new. In fact, Scriven (1967) proposed the terms *formative* and *summative assessments* to explain the two distinct roles in evaluating curriculum. Bloom (1971, 1976) took the term further and suggested that the same distinction be made in the evaluation of student learning. There is a long history within the research base for formative assessment that stems from Bloom's (1977) identification of two essential elements of formative learning. These elements are feedback for students and corrective conditions for all important components of learning, which has led to differentiated instruction. In 1988, Crooks' research identified classroom assessment practices on student learning and found that formative assessment is one of the most powerful tools for improving student learning and motivation. Both Ramaprasad (1983) and Sadler (1989) highlight the critical nature and importance of students monitoring their own learning as teachers provide feedback given as an essential element of formative assessment. This feedback loop is essential to helping students become metacognitive of any gaps or missing information in their learning process. As the research on formative assessment continued to escalate over the years, a major study by Black and Wiliam (1998) found evidence that formative assessment is an essential component of classroom work and that its development can raise standards of achievement. In 1998, they defined formative assessment as "encompassing all those activities undertaken by teachers, and/or by their students, which provide information to be used as feedback to modify the teaching and learning activities in which they are engaged." More recently, Wiliam (2011) states that "formative assessment practices appear to have a much greater impact on educational achievement than most other reforms."

The term *formative assessment* has built within it the merging of instruction with assessment. Shepard, Hammerness, Darling-Hammond & Rust (2005) discuss that the assessments are carried out during the teaching process for the purpose of informing and improving teaching or learning. Inherent in the word "formative" is formation, thus the forming of learning during instruction. Important in the formative assessment history occurred in 2006 when the Council of Chief State School Officers (CCSSO) made formative assessment an important emphasis in their adopted definition: "formative assessment is a process used by teachers and students during instruction that provides feedback to adjust ongoing teaching and learning to improve students' achievement of intended instructional outcomes" (CCSSO, 2008).

At-a-Glance: Historical Timeline of Formative Assessment

1967: Scriven created the terms formative and summative for evaluation.

1971, 1977: Bloom took the terms formative and summative into the classroom.

1989: Sadler emphasized student monitoring and feedback.

1998: Black and Wiliam highlight formative assessment in raising student achievement.

2006: The Council of Chief State School Officers (CCSSO) endorses formative assessment.

2011: Wiliam states that formative assessment has a greater impact on learning than other school reforms.

Like formative assessment, balanced literacy is not a new concept and has evolved from ideas of balanced approaches and instruction. The designation of balanced literacy originated in California in 1996 (California Department of Education, 1996; Honig, 1996; Asselin, 1999) and has a long history, which grew out of the reading wars and debates about how best to teach reading (Tompkins, 2013). Balanced literacy is a philosophical orientation that assumes reading and writing achievement are developed through instruction and support in multiple environments in which teachers use various approaches that differ by level of teacher support and child control (Frey, et al, 2005; Fountas & Pinnell, 1996). This philosophical orientation or perspective means that there is not one right approach to teaching reading (Fitzgerald, 1999), but rather a balanced approach to literacy development. An essential element within the balanced literacy pedagogy is that the teacher is making decisions moment by moment on the best ways to proceed with the instruction. This deliberate decision-making by the teacher forms the basis for daily instruction and is guided by the formative assessment process. Pearson (2002) discusses an ecologically balanced approach as one that "retains the practices that have proved useful from each era but transforms and extends them, rendering them more effective, more useful, and more supportive of teachers and students." He further states that this balanced approach will utilize authentic texts and tasks with heavy emphasis on writing, comprehension, reader response, and literature. It also includes phonics, word identification, spelling, and writing. Classroom instruction typically includes a daily literacy routine of read-alouds, guided reading, language walls, language and literacy centers, and independent reading and writing. Another viewpoint surrounding balanced literacy is that it centers on best practices, while staying away from the earlier debates, in a more flexible manner. That is, there are many independent aspects of literacy that must be simultaneously balanced (Madda, Griffo, Pearson & Raphael, 2007). For example, in a balanced literacy classroom, a teacher could be working with a small guided reading group and within the group could be differentiating instruction for each student. At the same time, the teacher is also keenly aware and observing students working independently at centers and reading and writing independently. Most recently, Tompkins (2010, 2013) describes the balanced approach to instruction as "a comprehensive view of literacy that combines explicit instruction, guided practice, collaborative learning, and independent reading and writing," all developed through instruction and support in multiple environments.

Within balanced literacy, there are key components that include the home and community, library involvement, structured classroom plans, read-alouds, guided reading, shared reading, and independent reading and writing (Fountas & Pinnell, 1996). Cunningham and Allington (2007) recommend that teachers use a balanced literacy approach that combines explicit instruction in decoding, fluency, vocabulary, comprehension, and writing, along with daily opportunities for students to apply what they are learning in authentic literacy activities. This could mean that when a teacher is working with a small group in guided reading, deliberate decisions about the needs of the children and the formation of knowledge and skills would be taken into real-time account. The teacher might work on decoding with some, fluency with others, and comprehension with all of the children through a combination of explicit instruction. At each point of instruction, the teacher is collecting formative data on each student's process of learning. This deliberate decision-making is a perfect example of how balanced literacy instruction merges with formative assessment, causing a perfect confluence of differentiated pedagogy. Understanding how children learn best and what instructional practices influence reading and writing must be considered as a basis for school-wide transformational change. Cohen and Cowen (2011) state that the primary goal of a balanced literacy program is not to teach reading as a skill broken into isolated steps, but as a lifelong learning process that promotes higher-order thinking, problem solving, and reasoning. Learning theories that support a student-centered balanced literacy classroom include constructivist theory (Smith, 2004), sociolinguistics (Vygotsky, 1978), and cognitive/information processing (Tracey and Morrow, 2006).

Language as a Lens for Formative Assessment

Most recently, Dargusch (2014) discusses formative assessment as a sociocultural framework, highlighting the ideas that it is social, situated, context bound, and context specific. For example, this means that during formative assessment within a classroom setting, the culture of the community and how children relate to and interact with each other and the teacher are important within the context. Interaction in this context includes parents and school administrators as well. We believe that language is a key contributing factor in the entire formative assessment framework described and influences literacy development and instruction. Paramount to student success is deliberately re-examining best practices in literacy instruction with a powerful new lens and shift of awareness to language development (which incorporates language as action, language and learning as social cognition and discourse, etc.). The term *discourse* is seen prominently in the academic language portion of the Common Core instructional shifts. Unfortunately, practicing teachers have had little preparation for this concept and are often unclear about the implementation of discourse into instruction (Policastro & McTague, 2015). Gee (2001) defines discourses as "ways of combining and coordinating words, deeds, thoughts, values, bodies, objects, tools, technologies, and other people so as to enact and recognize specific socially situated identities and activities."

Classroom discourse typically refers to the language that students and teachers use to communicate with each other, including talking, discussions, conversations, and debates. Although this is a complex term to understand and put into classroom use, Ruddell and Unrau (2004) explain that classroom discourse is about creating an abundance of oral texts that the students and the teacher interpret. This interpretation of how to comprehend the message, the source of the message, and the truth or correctness of the message is central to classroom discourse. As you can imagine, these forms of discourse take on many different formats within the classroom setting (such as large- and small-group instruction or students working in pairs) and are all paramount to all classroom conversations.

Classroom Discourse and Shared Talking

Throughout the tenets of the balanced literacy classroom, discourse is seen as a way in which to engage children in conversations, discussions, and classroom talk. Balanced literacy classrooms provide the optimal opportunity for children to learn about talking. They learn by talking and through talking, trying out ideas, and listening to others. Learning how to participate in this important classroom context allows them to understand themselves and the world (Pantaleo, 2007). We believe that classroom discourse is about shared talking that happens during the tenets of balanced literacy. The notions of shared talking are illuminated in a balanced literacy classroom. Children are interacting with one another and having stimulating discussions around the topics of instruction. This talking and listening is not only respected within the classroom culture but encouraged as an important component of the lesson. This does require the teacher to step back and allow for the students to do the talking while the teacher facilitates and observes, collecting important information and data from the students. Shared talking happens before, during, and after the interactive read-alouds. It occurs during guiding language into reading while the teacher facilitates shared talk before, during, and after work with the reading selection. During language and literacy center time, students have opportunities to solve problems and work on projects with peers where shared talk is expected and respected in the community. During independent reading and writing, learners have opportunities to discuss what they are reading and writing with their classmates. During these times, they have an opportunity to learn how to talk about literature and their responses to it.

In a balanced literacy classroom, noise levels will vary depending on the activity in progress. We have seen some successful management strategies where teachers use a green, yellow, and red system for gauging the levels of noise. The teacher has these circles visible for the class to see. When the green circle is up, the noise level is good; yellow means caution, indicating that the noise level is increasing; and red means that the level of noise must come down immediately. Students get used to this system, and there is little time taken for the adjustments to the levels when it is in place. Noise levels are established as a class and cover the following: working with a partner, working independently, working in a small group, and working with the teacher.

Language Walls and Shared Talking

In *The New Balanced Literacy School: Implementing Common Core*, we introduce the idea of moving from word walls to language walls. When using language walls, word walls expand to a more sophisticated level and larger unit of thought to include ideas, notions, images, and much more from a text, allowing for rich conversations and discussions during shared talking. Language walls allow for both social and classroom discourse to happen and let the teacher document certain aspects of language. Shared talking now moves to the language wall where thoughts and ideas can be visual and connections can be made.

These language walls are ongoing within classrooms and evolve on a daily basis. Dry-erase boards work well and allow for a tremendous amount of language to transpire during the course of a day. We have found that teachers who have transitioned from word walls to language walls are provided with added flexibility in teaching a lesson. The language and discourse grows and evolves within the lesson, forever changing and transitioning into the next discourse study. Language walls can also be used in physical education (PE), art, music, and math classes.

What Does Formative Assessment Look Like in the New Balanced Literacy Classroom?

There are three major processes in the formative assessment classroom that begin with the learning goal or purpose of the lesson and incorporate the following:

1. Formative collection of data,
2. Formative feedback to the student, and
3. Formative self-monitoring by the student of his/her learning.

These assessment processes form the structure for the formation of knowledge and skills in a balanced literacy classroom. These formative assessment processes are not discrete nor are they individually distinct or separate from each other. Rather, they are very much connected, joined, and linked together within daily instruction. Within the formative assessment process of collecting data, providing feedback to students, and helping them monitor their learning are interactive in nature. For example, during a conference with a student about her writing, the teacher might be giving both verbal and written feedback, notating the student's self-monitoring and collecting other pertinent data on the student. We do not want this process to be perceived as a step 1, step 2, and step 3. Rather, it is an ongoing and continuous cycle of instruction. However, there are certain things that need to happen to get ready for formative assessment in a balanced literacy classroom. This includes developing a routine for each of the tenets of balanced literacy to get the most out of the formative assessment process. Additionally, a critical dimension includes the process whereby this formation of knowledge goes home in real time; that is, formative assessments go home. This is an important component as communication in an ongoing manner to parents is essential in the literacy learning process. (See Chapter Seven.)

The Thinking Notes Circle at right was created as a visual reminder for the teacher to deliberately be thinking about formative collection, feedback, and self-monitoring during all aspects of balanced literacy. One teacher told us that she uses this circle on a daily basis and leaves it on her clipboard as a reminder to take formative collection notes on each tenet of balanced literacy. We really like the idea of keeping formative thinking notes during instruction. We developed a 110 Minutes of Daily Balanced Literacy routine centered on the tenets of balanced literacy. Each of the tenets will be described (read-aloud, guiding language into reading, language and literacy centers, and independent reading and writing) in detail with suggestions for note taking in Chapters Two, Three, Four, and Five. Each of the tenets of balanced literacy will be highlighted to show how formative assessment works within each.

Thinking Notes
Circle

Read-alouds

Guided Reading

Language & Literacy Centers

Independent Reading & Writing

Our new balanced literacy model merges the new instructional shifts necessary for student success. Now more than ever, particular attention needs to be on formative assessment. Popham (2008) states, "Formative assessment represents evidenced-based instructional decision-making. If you want to become more instructionally effective and if you want your students to achieve more, then formative assessment should be for you." This certainly captures the essence of how balanced literacy and formative assessment are the perfect confluence. The three assessment processes form the structure for the formation of knowledge and skills in a balanced literacy classroom. Once a learning goal or purpose of the balanced literacy lesson has been established, the process can begin. Formative collection, feedback, and self-monitoring all interact with and inform each other.

The Formative Assessment Process

The formative assessment process begins with the goal or purpose of the lesson. Fisher and Frey (2010) state that each lesson "should have a purpose," and that purpose should be clearly articulated to focus on instruction and providing students with the answer to the question of why they have to learn this. Fisher and Frey also contend that communicating the purpose to students is a must. There are several ways in which this can be done. Some teachers post this purpose on the board or on an easel next to the group, and others discuss the purpose with the children and then have them write it down in their own words. Heritage (2011) states that formative assessment is only effective when teachers are clear about the intended learning goals for the lesson. We love walking into a classroom and knowing immediately what the purpose of the lesson is. Awareness of the purpose is essential if we want students to build their metacognitive and self-monitoring skills. If they are not aware of the purpose, they can't self-monitor their learning.

Date: _____

🌂 Student Tool: Purpose Card

The purpose of the lesson today is:

_____

_____

_____

_____

Identify the Purpose

Guiding Questions:

- Do you set a purpose for each of your lessons?

- Do you communicate and review the purpose of the lesson with the students?

- Do you post the purpose of the lesson so the students can see it?

- Where do you post the purpose of the lesson?

- Do students get to write down the purpose of the lesson in their own words?

Allowing students time to write the purpose before the lesson is a good way for them to be aware of the exact aim of the learning. This would not have to be done for every single lesson, but when a new unit is beginning, it will take several days or weeks to complete the purpose. For each of the tenets of balanced literacy, posting the purpose of the lesson will make responsibilities clear to the community. During read-alouds and guiding language into reading, the purpose could be posted on an easel next to where the group is sitting. For language and literacy centers, the purpose of the lesson must be posted at the center with clear guidelines and directions for how to achieve the learning purpose. For independent reading and writing, the purpose might be posted in the classroom community or different purposes might be established for different students. These purposes could be articulated and communicated during conference time, when the student could then write the learning purpose within his or her reading/writing notebook. We think it is important that the teacher refers to the purpose frequently during and after the lessons.

Examples of Lesson Purposes

Read-Aloud: Create a chronological timeline of events from the text.

Guiding Language into Reading: Identify the characters, setting, problem, and solution to the story.

Language and Literacy Centers: Report on a topic in an organized manner using facts and descriptive details to support the main idea.

Independent Reading and Writing: Write a summary of the information that you read.

The model below shows the three processes within formative assessment. The teacher collects formative data on all gaps in student learning, along with assessing the lesson goals and purposes. Formative feedback is provided in real time and moves the student forward in his or her learning. Formative monitoring takes place as students self-assess and monitor their learning. Teachers provide feedback to the students regarding their self-monitoring skills.

The Formative Assessment Process Framework

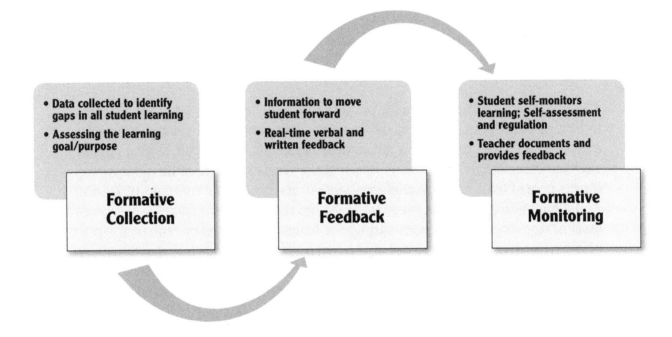

- Data collected to identify gaps in all student learning
- Assessing the learning goal/purpose

Formative Collection

- Information to move student forward
- Real-time verbal and written feedback

Formative Feedback

- Student self-monitors learning; Self-assessment and regulation
- Teacher documents and provides feedback

Formative Monitoring

Formative Collection

During the instructional process, teachers are observing and noticing students' reactions, responses, and decision-making within problem solving along with many other behaviors within the continuum of the learning process. Fisher and Frey (2014) state that formative assessment must begin with the "learning target," which would include what the students should know and be able to do during the lesson. Often teachers use an array of strategies to collect data on these learning targets. (See 26 Formative Assessment Strategies starting on page 158 for a list.) Some might include teacher-made checklists, informal assessments, or anecdotal records. Heritage (2011) refers to these as "evidence collection" that should yield information that is actionable by the teacher and student. She also believes that this evidence collection must be systematic and a planned activity. These forms of collection might be used during the literacy routine. For example, during a guided reading lesson, a teacher observes students responding to questions. These responses are noted by the teacher. A special notation might be made because a student, who has not participated in discussions, now actively participates, indicating a learning gap that is closing. During independent reading, a student might be engaged in a text and showing signs that the text is too difficult. In both of these situations, collecting student data is essential to the students' ability to progress. Helping students "fill in the gap" in learning is critical to the collection process. This learning gap is thought of as missing pieces of information that the student needs to learn for the desired goal to be reached (Sadler, 1989). Roskos and Neuman (2012) refer to this as the "Gap Minder," or identifying the gap between where students are and where they need to go in their development. This gap in learning is meant to propel all students forward, including high achievers. This model does not have a ceiling on learning; rather, it is meant to differentiate the instruction to further the continued learning for all students.

Within the new balanced literacy model, teachers have opportunities to collect data on students during read-alouds, guiding language into reading, center time, and independent reading and writing. Collection of this student data allows the teacher to document the formation of knowledge and skills necessary to be successful as a reader and writer. We believe it is essential for students to know what is expected of them during the literacy lesson and what they should be aware of. The collection of formative data by the teacher will highlight this process. We also believe that part of the collection of formative data might arise from unanticipated responses, behaviors, and outcomes that might not necessarily be connected to the learning goal. Fletcher (2013) describes this as incidental or spur-of-the-moment formative assessments, which can be quite effective for monitoring learning in real time. Students surprise us all the time in their learning process, and we must be both open and welcome to documenting and collecting information that is indirectly part of the purpose of the lesson. We cannot lose sight of the purpose of the lesson; we just accept and expect the unanticipated. For example, you have probably asked a question about the text during a guided reading lesson and had a student make a connection to his life and then connect it back to the classroom. That is an unexpected—but certainly welcome—moment!

We realize that not all data or information on a learner will be written down. Teaching is ongoing, and there are many moments in which the teacher is teaching and responding to the learner based on incoming information in the moment. However, we do believe that the reflective process of teaching and formative assessment will promote written information by the teacher, especially when it is noteworthy.

Formative Feedback

Lin and Lai (2013) discuss feedback in the following manner: "Formative assessments, continuously embedded in the teaching and learning process of a curriculum, attempt to improve learning achievements by offering feedback in the process." What makes this interesting is they show how feedback is integrated into improving the learning process. Hattie and Timperley (2007) state that feedback is one of the most powerful influences on learning and achievement but the result can be either positive or negative on the student. They discuss that providing feedback requires high-level thinking by both the teachers and students, making it clear that feedback is not merely a "stimulus and response" model but requires a sophisticated class culture or climate. We want to differentiate the difference between "feedback" and "formative feedback." Feedback that compliments or criticizes work done by a student is not "formative feedback." Wiliam (2011) states that the formative feedback provided to the learner must cause a "cognitive" response not an "emotional" response. Cognitive responses will propel the learner forward, while an emotional response will cause a different kind of response. If the feedback is critical in nature without directions on how to move forward, the learner may not be motivated to continue on.

Example of feedback that causes a cognitive response: "You did a fine job of finding evidence from the text. Your next steps are to begin building an argument from the evidence. After you have established an argument, begin working on how this will be presented in a debate."

Example of feedback that causes an emotional response: "I am disappointed in your work. I know that you could have done a better job on this task."

The first response is a formative feedback example that identifies for the student exactly what he has correctly accomplished and then provides the next steps that need to be taken in order to keep the learning moving forward. This involves the thinking or a cognitive response. In the second response, the student is not provided with information on how to move forward with the learning process. Rather, this response is more than likely to result in or elicit an emotional response from the learner.

When we think of formative assessment merging with instruction into a formative learning process, feedback becomes the vehicle that can drive instruction.

During reflective assessment, decision-making and instruction adjustments are made by the teacher and learning adjustments are made by the student. Within this feedback setting, a teacher must be able to implement and deal with the complexities of multiple judgments required in the feedback process. This includes a deep understanding of the content area of the lesson and the ability to provide feedback about tasks before students get discouraged, feel frustrated, or fall behind. The Council of Chief State School Officers (CCSSO, 2008) states that descriptive and timely feedback should be based on the learning goal and help the students answer three basic questions: Where am I going? Where am I now? How I can I close the gap? Sadler (1998) stresses that formative feedback does make a difference, and it is not the quantity of feedback that is critical, but rather the quality of feedback. Sadler suggests that an important dimension of quality formative feedback is communication that brings confidence and hope and inspires the learner to move forward. For example, if a student is working on a piece of writing and does not get feedback that encourages her to move forward, it is not formative feedback. This might happen when a writing assignment is returned to a student, and grammar and spelling errors are highlighted with no real feedback to improve performance. We see many written products that involve this type of feedback and it is not formative. Rather than marking grammatical or spelling errors, the teacher should give the student a clear path of how to achieve the improved grammar and spelling, such as using a spelling- and grammar-checking program on the computer. This would also free up feedback from the teacher to focus on the content instead.

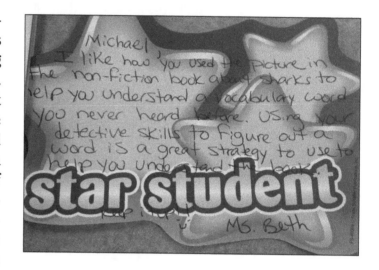

Wiliam (2011) defines formative feedback as the following:

- "Feedback functions formatively only if the information fed back to the learner is used by the learner in improving performance."
- "If the information fed back to the learner is intended to be helpful but cannot be used by the learner in improving performance, it is not formative."
- "Feedback must embody a model of progression whereby a series of activities must be designed to move the learner from current state to goal state."
- "We need to ensure that feedback causes a cognitive rather than an emotional reaction." (It is not a compliment or a criticism.)
- "The purpose of feedback should be to increase the extent to which students are owners of their own learning."

Feedback must be delivered in both oral (verbal) and written forms. Verbal feedback is important during the moment-by-moment teaching, whether it is large-group, small-group, or one-on-one instruction. The power of verbal feedback as part of the discussion or conference allows students to receive information immediately. By providing this timely form of feedback, students receive the information within the context of the lesson, allowing for a continuous process and flow embedded in instruction. Written feedback follows verbal feedback, providing reflections from the teacher with the goal of moving/guiding the student further in the learning process.

Guided Feedback

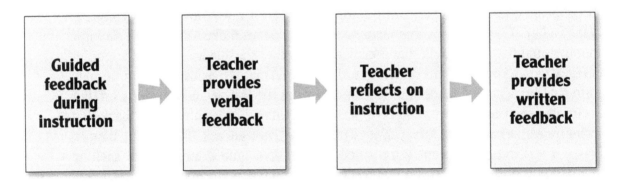

Providing feedback to learners as soon as possible allows for real-time processing. When real-time or timely feedback occurs, students begin to expect it. We observed in our clinic that when teachers posted written feedback in student journals, students came in each morning looking for the feedback. This propelled them forward in their next journal entry.

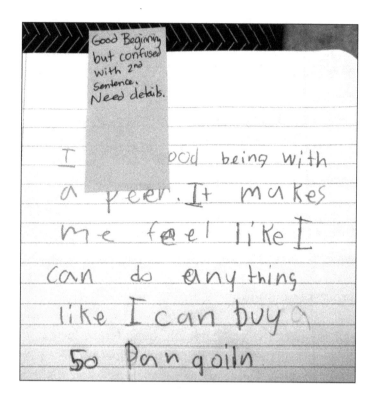

Delaying feedback to the learner can be costly in terms of moving the learner forward. We know that feedback occurring only during parent-teacher conferences is not enough. Often the information provided is outdated as the learner has progressed since the information was collected.

We would like to promote timely feedback as part of the ongoing process of instruction. Feedback functions as a way to help students monitor every aspect of their learning. No doubt, some feedback is intended and can benefit all students. This can be done during live instruction. For example, during a guided reading lesson, the teacher might give feedback that redirects the students' thinking to a particular response. This might include pointing to a picture or giving them feedback clues to guide and support their thinking. Verbal feedback through conversations as part of conferencing can be molded and shaped into feedback that moves the students forward in their learning. This requires a special lens or reflection on instruction with the primary goal of continuously moving students forward in their learning. Sometimes it is easier to understand a concept when it is put into a different situation. Learning how to ride a bike is a good metaphor for feedback in the classroom. That is, if the child learning how to ride a bike does not get immediate feedback, she could fall down. When getting feedback on how to steer, peddle, grip, and so forth, the rider can process the information immediately and move forward. Likewise, if the student had to wait for feedback, the learning process would be broken and disjointed. Immediate feedback can be provided to whole groups, small groups, and individual students.

- How often do you give feedback?

- Do you give verbal feedback during instruction?
  To the whole group? Small group? One on one?

- When do you follow up with written feedback?

- How is the timing of your feedback?

Written feedback functions differently from verbal feedback as the teacher has had time to reflect on the instruction and put the feedback into a visible form. Written feedback takes the invisible oral comments and allows them to be tangible and something students can see and respond to over time. Verbal feedback is necessary and begins the process of monitoring learning by the student.

The timing and frequency of feedback will be different for each of the tenets of balanced literacy. When teachers are collecting information for each tenet, there will be times when verbal feedback is immediate, such as when it's given to the whole group during a read-aloud or a small group during guided reading. Written feedback might take longer as the teacher needs to process and reflect on the information.

It is also important to feature student work both in the classroom and hallways, providing a way to share the feedback in the community. This manner in which feedback is conveyed and displayed contributes to creating a climate and culture of feedback. We recently visited a kindergarten classroom where the teacher had displayed the children's writing with detailed formative feedback in the hallway. The teacher explained that aside from sharing student work with the school, this was also a way to communicate with the parents. In our clinic, we have had success with this approach. Students enjoyed reading their own feedback and others' in the hallway. We want to also add that this feedback is informative to all the students as they gain insights into how they can be moved forward in their learning. This public display of formative feedback requires a climate and culture where it is accepted and expected by all in the community. This requires capacity building where collaboration, trust, and willingness to share are a priority.

Most recently, we visited a school where the bulletin board outside the principal's office featured student work. This is a common practice in many schools. As the school has evolved into a balanced literacy school with professional development centered on formative assessment, this principal now writes formative feedback and displays this on the student work. This is another example of the formative feedback going public within the community.

Formative Self-Monitoring

One of the most important outcomes of formative assessment is that students learn to monitor their own processes. Hudesman, Crosby, Flugman, Isaac, Everson, and Clay (2013) report that "The research we have reported on, when taken together with an ever growing body of other work, has demonstrated the importance of integrating formative assessment and metacognition with academic content instruction so that students can optimize their learning." Indeed, metacognition plays a vital role in learners' self-knowledge, regulation, and monitoring of their thought processes (Policastro, 1993). Marcell (2007) describes metacognition as the ultimate goal of the reading process. As with formative assessment and balanced literacy, there exists a rich history on metacognition beginning with Flavell (1976), who introduced the theoretical construct to explain one's knowledge, self-awareness, and monitoring concerning one's own cognitive processes, strengths, and weaknesses. Additionally, the term *metacognition* refers to controlling one's own learning or self-regulation and monitoring these behaviors (Baker & Brown, 1984).

An example of a metacognitive experience is when a reader stops, wonders, and self-questions. It is through this act that the student determines whether the selection needs to be reread for complete comprehension. A student lacking these self-monitoring or metacognitive skills would continue to read a selection without understanding the text being read. The student fails to self-monitor and ask the question "Is what I am reading making sense?" When students are provided with real-time support on strategy use, they know the appropriate strategy is to reread the information or stop reading because the text is too difficult. Wang and Palinscar (1989) defined metacognition as "the students' ability to assume an active role in their learning as self-instructive." Keeley (2013) brings forth the reflective nature of metacognition as providing an opportunity for students to recognize how their thinking has changed as a result of their instructional experiences. She states, "Formative assessment is also used at the end of a sequence of instruction to provide an opportunity for students to refine their thinking and reflect back on how their ideas have changed." In the sample on the next page, the student was asked to reflect on what ways he improved in the first quarter of the school year and the goals he would like to achieve in the second quarter. Finally, the student was asked to comment on what to do if he feels restless in class. We think the written responses show an abundance of self-monitoring skills on the student's part, indicating his ability to take an active role.

> 1. I have improved a lot. In the begining of the quarter I was not good. But then I got better. Now there are some days I am good and some days I am not. I also am geting better in academic things like Math, spelling, and gym.
> 2. The goals that I would like to achieve are not to get into a lot of trouble. Not to upset other kids.
> 3. I find myself restless when teachers talk and talk and talk and
> talk also during times when I can not talk about the subject we are all talking about. A way I could prevent my self from geting into trouble is I could clap 2 and get up softly and go out into the ha and get a drink of water and softly come back in.

Inherent within the formative assessment model are students becoming owners of their own learning. This ownership requires students to reflect on and monitor their learning during instruction. Self-monitoring requires students to use self-questioning, self-observation, and self-coaching. These forms of inner language are often referred to as self-talk (Manning & Payne, 1996; Spencer, 2001; Purkey, 2002), or a person's interior dialogue. Fisher and Frey (2008) refer to self-talk as purposeful student talk that is an independent task. This inner language is prominent with the self-monitoring metacognitive skills of the students. This aspect of formative assessment highlights the internal language and dialogue that is going on inside students' minds. Teachers need to pay attention to the internal dialogue and language of the student. Tapping into the internal dialogue of students is import as it allows the teacher to begin to understand the thought processes surrounding literacy. Often students are thinking about important aspects of their learning but not expressing it. When we allow students to share what they are thinking, we get insights into the most important cognitive process. Teachers can model this kind of behavior when they share their internal dialogue out loud with students; often referred to as *think-alouds*. Thus, this self-talk plays an important role in the students' own learning process. In the sample interview on page 39, a student is able to identify when he self-talks during school and specifically during literacy activities.

Self-Assessment and Self-Talk Interview and Feedback

Do you ever talk to yourself in school? Well, sometimes during computer time, I say, like, "Let's play this game" or "Let's play that game."

Tell me more about when you do that. Give me some other real examples of when you self-talk in school. Well, like, during a spelling test. I remember the words from some place in my house. I say, like, "I know this has to be right because I remember where I was when I studied this word with my mom."

Do you ever talk to yourself when you are reading or writing? Well, for reading, I don't know, but for writing, I say "Is this what I should be writing?"

Can you give me some real examples? Well, like, during writer's workshop, the teacher always says, like, make sure what you're writing makes sense to another person—read it to your partner to make sure. Well, I say to myself—"Gee, I want to see if it makes sense to me first." So I always read it to see if it makes sense. Then I let my partner read it over.

Feedback to student: I really like how you self-question as you go through your school day. Keep asking yourself those questions as you read and write. This is an excellent way to keep track of your learning, and this is exactly what good readers and writers do.

Other ways that teachers can elicit this internal dialogue during instruction is to model the behaviors and then ask students for their own ideas. For example, the teacher might share the following: "During the read-aloud, I said to myself that I did not know about the events in the country where the story takes place." During guided reading, the teacher might talk about his/her life as a reader: "When I am reading, I often say to myself that I need to reread a passage several times to really make sure that I understand it." And during independent writing time, the teacher might say "When writing in my journal, I ask myself what important experiences have happened lately that I can write about." During one recent classroom visit, we observed the teacher asking the children "Are we on or off task?" The children all responded that they were off task. The teacher then asked "What do we say to ourselves?" The children all responded "Get back on task." Again, this is a nice example of the teacher promoting the use of self-talk as a way to monitor the learning process.

Little did we realize that this pioneer work on metacognition would have such a powerful impact on the formative assessment process. Metacognition has played a key role throughout the years, but it is the formative assessment process that aligns it with the learning and instruction process. Often, this self-monitoring is seen as an important skill for students but viewed in the classroom as separate from the ongoing learning and instructional process. What makes this difficult for practice is that metacognition is often seen as a theoretical concept and not easily adapted for the classroom. Going from theory to practice is not always easy, and formative assessment, along with the tenets of balanced literacy, provides the bridge to take teachers and students from a concept to implementation. As part of formative assessment, students will be monitoring their own learning. Teachers need to be keenly aware of and document when students are self-regulating their knowledge. Students should receive feedback on their regulation of their learning.

According to Andrade and Valtcheva (2009), "self-assessment is a process of formative assessment during which students reflect on the quality of their work, judge the degree to which it reflects explicitly stated goals or criteria, and revise accordingly." Teaching students to self-assess or monitor their own learning is a key component of formative assessment, and it is something that we can do in classrooms. Some students can do this naturally and know immediately if they do not understand something. Self-monitoring and assessing of learning is something that good readers and writers do on their own. The good news is that this can be taught to students who don't yet do this on their own. Learning how to self-assess during instruction is central to the instructional process. This process will require modeling of questions and showing students how to keep track of their own learning and understanding. Panadero and Alonso-Tapia (2013) have outlined five instructional aides to promote self-assessment as follows:

1. Self-assessment modeling,
2. Direct instruction and assistance for self-assessment,
3. Cues that help to know when it is appropriate to self-assess,
4. Practice, and
5. Opportunities to review and improve the process of realizing the task as well as the final performance.

For each of the tenets of balanced literacy, we want students to be conscious of their learning process. One place to begin is by having daily conversations about self-assessment and making it part of daily literacy routines. For example, when a teacher begins a guided reading lesson with a small group of children, there are students working at centers and there is a discussion about the self-assessment. In other words, the lessons now include a self-monitoring component—students are aware of it and expect it. This self-monitoring is built into each lesson.

Instrumental in this process is that teachers need to provide students feedback regarding their self-monitoring. For example, feedback could be given during one-on-one or small-group conferencing when the teacher and student have an opportunity to review work. We like the idea of students keeping track of their learning in a self-monitoring notebook. This notebook could have a tab for each of the tenets of balanced literacy (read-alouds, guided reading, centers, and independent reading and writing). Although language walls and multiple in-school libraries are considered tenets of our new balanced literacy model, they will be discussed later as language walls can evolve and grow out from read-alouds, guided reading, centers, and independent reading and writing. Access to books through the libraries is needed to provide the balanced literacy instruction that merges with formative assessment. This management notebook allows for students to keep track of their learning on a daily basis.

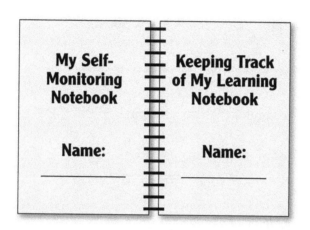

With a self-monitoring notebook, teachers could be sure to model and give directions on each of the forms to students. At the end of Chapters Two, Three, Four, and Five are formative assessment forms for the teacher and self-monitoring forms for students. There are forms for each of the tenets of balanced literacy. These forms are not grade specific and will need to be tailored to meet the needs of each classroom teacher. Although we have provided several forms from which to choose, we do think that the best way to implement classroom formative assessment is for each teacher to develop his or her own system with forms for collection of data, feedback to students, and student self-monitoring. Our materials may be a good starting place for continued feedback.

Research shows that children need a lot of practice in self-monitoring. The student tools will provide the needed and necessary practice in self-monitoring of learning. These forms could be put into notebooks as a way to manage this aspect of formative assessment. Keeping these in a notebook is also perfect for sharing with parents. Formative assessment should be frequently shared with parents. (See Chapter Seven for more information on communicating with parents.) A notebook could also allow students to take it home and review it with their parents. This notebook could also serve as a nice addition during the parent-teacher conference. This notebook could be created for use on the computer as well. Students could have access to these forms and keep them in a document for easy access.

Teaching Students to Self-Monitor

1. Discuss self-assessment before, during, and after instruction.
2. Provide models and give specific directions for self-assessments.
3. Show students how to self-assess with step-by-step modeling.
4. Provide feedback to students on self-assessment.
5. Have lots of practice with self-assessment.
6. Create self-monitoring notebooks for students.

Guiding Questions:

- Do you help students monitor their own learning during instruction?
- How do you help students monitor their own learning?

A Framework for Balanced Literacy, CCSS Instructional Shifts, and Formative Assessment

In *The New Balanced Literacy School: Implementing Common Core*, we explain that balanced literacy has been influenced by three instructional shifts described by Achieve (2012) and the eight big shifts described by Tim Shanahan (2013). We then took each of the shifts and changes necessary for success with CCSS and aligned them with the tenets of balanced literacy. The table on the next couple pages explains how formative assessment may be combined with balanced literacy and the CCSS instructional shifts into one implementation model.

The New Balanced Literacy	CCSS Instructional Shifts	Formative Assessment
The New Read-Aloud	The new read-aloud reflects the language of learners. Fifty percent of the texts used in kindergarten through fifth grade are exemplar informational and complex texts, and the percent increases to 70 for grades six through 12. The read-alouds include all content areas and poetry while modeling close reading, repeated readings, and written responses. Teachers make inter-textual connections, use academic vocabulary within the social discourse, and have rigorous conversations. Language is in action during read-alouds.	Teachers use the following for formative collection of data: observation, anecdotal notes, interactive read-aloud strategies with individual whiteboards, read-aloud listening checklist, follow-up journal writing entries, responses to teacher questions, and exit slips. Teachers respond to students with formative feedback in both written and oral formats. Students monitor their formation of learning through metacognitive processes.
The New Guiding Language into Reading	The new guided reading/writing includes guiding language into literacy as a staircase of complexity and uses language to guide, scaffold, and inform all literacy instruction, including phonemic awareness through comprehension, close readings, and repeated readings, with 50 percent informational and complex text. Teachers guide students into developing text-based answers and habits of evidentiary arguments through social discourse and academic vocabulary. Book club serves as a way to guide language into reading, especially in the intermediate and upper grades. Students are guided through 21st century research and communication tools.	Teacher is "clipboard ready" to collect data by taking observational and anecdotal notes. Teacher checklists and inventories are utilized, along with running records, as part of guided reading. Student data is collected during lesson discourse, and the teacher confers with small groups and individual students on oral and written responses. Teacher provides real-time feedback to students. Students monitor their learning through metacognitive processes.

The New Balanced Literacy	CCSS Instructional Shifts	Formative Assessment
Language and Literacy Centers	Center projects can include solving problems, reading with a partner, raising issues, writing research reports, generating discussions, preparing research presentations, and building arguments and persuasion individually and in teams. These projects revolve around using 21st century research and communication tools.	Teacher observes students working independently and with partners at centers. Student data is collected, analyzed, and used as evidence of progress toward learning. Formative feedback is provided and students self-monitor their learning.
Independent Reading and Writing	A balance of informational and disciplinary literacy texts (science, social studies, etc.) helps students access the world of knowledge, read complex texts to find evidence and build knowledge, and read for different purposes. There is a focus on knowledge of language and language conventions for opinion and persuasion, generative, informative and explanatory, and narrative writing. Students participate in shared and peer research and writing and writing from text sources. Evidence to inform or make an argument is practiced as is compare and contrast. Students increase the time spent writing, increase motivation for writing, use technology, and write responses from discourse while implementing 21st century research and communication tools.	The formative collection of data occurs through teacher observations and checklists, student conferencing, and portfolios. Students receive formative feedback and self-monitor their learning.

In the next few chapters, we will provide step-by-step instructions that provide more detail on each of these tenets.

Chapter Two: Formative Assessment: The New Read-Aloud

Guiding Questions:

- Why is reading aloud important for formative assessment?

- What is a read-aloud routine?

- How do I collect formative assessment data during a read-aloud?

- How do I provide formative feedback to students?

- How can students monitor their own learning during a read-aloud?

Reading Aloud and Formative Assessment: A Snapshot

Before the read-aloud, the teacher establishes the purpose of the lesson, the book to read, who the reader will be, and where the book will be read. The children anticipate the read-aloud and interact with one another. The teacher begins to observe keenly and collect important information before, during, and after the reading about the children's interest, enthusiasm, and much more. The information is collected mentally by the teacher and written down for documentation (see forms at the end of the chapter). For example, during the read-aloud, the teacher poses questions and the children could have an option to respond on whiteboards and share their answers. The teacher notates students' responses and interactions, providing instant feedback during the read-aloud. The teacher helps those students who need to make adjustments to their responses. After the read-aloud, time is set aside for students to self-assess and monitor their learning through exit slips. The teacher provides written feedback when necessary to students to assist with the purpose of the lesson.

Teacher Talk During Formative Assessment and Read-Aloud

- *The teacher talks about the purpose of the read-aloud and refers to the purpose often during the read-aloud, reminding students what is important to pay attention to ("Remember to pay attention to _____ ."). The teacher asks questions that relate to the purpose in order to assess children's knowledge. The teacher observes and collects data on students' understanding of the purpose of the lesson while providing feedback.*

- *The teacher talks about self-monitoring and how it is important to be aware of information that you don't understand. The teacher models, for example, "I didn't know the word _____ ." The teacher reminds students that this information is important to document on exit slips or other self-monitoring forms. (See forms at the end of the chapter.)*

- *The teacher stops and asks pertinent questions during the read-aloud and talks about making predictions, noticing character feelings, drawing conclusions, and finding evidence from the text. Students respond on whiteboards in words or with pictures. The teacher uses this opportunity to check for understanding and to assist students.*

- *The Teacher talks about and uses academic language, such as "Today we are going to be doing a lot of predicting as we read this story."*

- *The teacher talks to students about monitoring their responses on the whiteboards during a "turn-and-talk to your partner about your response." The teacher now moves through the group and listens and shares responses with the children, making note of responses.*

- *The teacher talks about making sure that responses are evidenced based on examples from the text.*

- *The teacher provides verbal feedback and confers with students as they respond to the questions.*

- *The teacher talks about and uses academic vocabulary before, during, and after the read-aloud: "Today we are going to spend time identifying the main idea of the story." The teacher talks about what identifying is and provides examples.*

There is no question that reading aloud to children is an important aspect of the balanced literacy classroom. We see teachers reading aloud daily to their students in most schools that we visit. In fact, the read-aloud is considered an integral aspect of the literacy block in many classrooms. What we have observed is that the read-aloud is in perfect alignment with formative assessment as it gives the teacher an opportunity to observe and document how a child responds to, interacts with, and listens to both fiction and nonfiction. We propose that the read-aloud become a high priority for collecting data on students, refocusing the lens of what and how we think about reading to our students. What makes the new read-aloud different from reading aloud in the past is that the teacher is making decisions surrounding the selection, questions, and overall instruction. The new read-aloud is also longer as the focus of the lesson is different from the past. The teacher stops more often to instruct, model close reading, and engage the children in serious conversations that invoke discourse. From this discourse, children have the opportunity to learn about developing arguments from the evidence in the selection that the teacher has read. The teacher may pause during the read-aloud to model a close reading behavior, which will draw the children's attention to certain aspects of the text and to specific details and information. The teacher continuously uses this time to check for understanding of the material.

We believe that the read-aloud is a valuable strategy for collecting pertinent and real-time data on students. Moreover, the read-aloud serves many purposes for collecting formative data. The read-aloud goes well beyond entertainment and enjoyment and moves toward a deeper appreciation of literature. This literature now includes both narrative and informational text. Teachers have the opportunity to document the formation of literacy skills during the read-aloud, provide feedback to students, and assist students in their own monitoring of their learning.

Selecting Texts to Read Aloud

Teachers make many decisions when selecting text for the read-aloud. One decision is whether to read nonfiction, informational text, or fiction. We have always been firm believers in reading aloud to children. However, it has been rather recent that we have seen the results of what happens when informational books are read aloud. Yopp and Yopp (2006) found that informational texts have not been made a priority. Rather, stories or narrative were the main selections teachers chose.

We encourage the development of a **read-aloud library** as part of the multiple in-school libraries. This library serves an important function for teachers to have access to a wide range of nonfiction and fiction books. With the emphasis on access to informational texts that align with the Common Core, we believe it is both essential and critical to incorporate informational texts into the daily read-alouds in all the elementary grades. In reviewing the literature, Andler (2014) states that nonfiction is also labeled as informational text and expository text. Duke (2003) defines informational texts as "texts that convey information about the natural world (such as fact books about snakes or trees) or the social world (such as books about building bridges or holiday customs)." Reading aloud informational texts to children is a wonderful way for them to learn about different genres and characteristics of the text. In our work, we have been amazed at young children's high levels of background knowledge on certain topics, such as animals, weather, traditions, and other countries, to name just a few. For older children, we have been surprised at their thirst and quest for this rich information. We have seen children in the upper grades ask for informational books to be read aloud. We have found that older children love to have informational texts read aloud—they are both engaged and absorbed by the content.

As discussed, the narrative was usually chosen for read-alouds, but informational text is engaging to students as well. Furthermore, Santoro, Chard, Howard, and Baker (2008) suggest that comprehension and vocabulary are promoted by using both narrative and informational text. They believe the read-aloud must go beyond enjoyment, be carefully planned, and incorporate both comprehension and vocabulary instruction.

Reading a narrative aloud provides opportunities for the teacher to formatively assess the comprehension of the story. For example teachers can assess students' ability to sequence events; identify the beginning, middle, and end or text structures, such as cause and effect; predict; identify feelings and emotions of the characters; give the main idea; and much more. Informational texts provide the opportunity for teachers to assess students' background knowledge on the subjects. They also provide a way to watch the formation of knowledge within the informational subjects progress and grow for the students.

A Routine for the Read-Aloud

Identify the learning purpose or target. There are many purposes for reading aloud, so the specific target must be stated before the read-aloud begins. We once saw a teacher state that the purpose was predicting what might happen next. The students were aware of the purpose and knew exactly what the lesson was about. We saw another teacher state specifically that the purpose was to follow the sequence and be able to retell the beginning, middle, and end of the story. In both instances, the purpose was written on a large easel next to where the teacher was reading. Establishing and identifying the purpose of the read-aloud lesson is the first aspect of this daily routine.

Greenstein (2010) explains that there is power in the pre-assessment routine as teachers need to find out what children know before beginning instruction. Further, she identifies this as the first and most crucial step in using formative assessment. This aspect of the routine can take the form of an informal pre-test to measure background knowledge and skills. While visiting a kindergarten class, we saw a teacher read *Bunny Cakes* by Rosemary Wells (Penguin, 1997) to the children. Before she began to read, she asked, "How many of you know this book?" More than half of the class of 20 children responded, and the children shared how they knew the book. Some said they had it at home and it was read to them, and others talked about reading it on their own. All of the responses indicated to the teacher that this was perhaps not new information for half of the class. Quick checks like this before previewing the book provide knowledge children may already have about a book.

> **Quick Check before the Read-Aloud**
>
> 1. How many of you know this book?
> 2. How many of you have read this book?
> 3. How many of you have this book at home?

Built into the daily routine should be time to enjoy and revel in the read-aloud. Children enjoy having a book read to them, and teachers can use this time to observe how the children respond to the selection. Some books are classroom favorites. In fact, we have seen classrooms where the previous and next read-aloud continues to be featured.

Document the read-alouds as they are completed. Keeping track, documenting, and archiving books read is an important dimension to the entire literacy routine. (See the documentation form on page 62.) We have found this documentation to be especially handy and helpful. This serves as a way to keep track of books read and a way to share with parents on a weekly basis what has been accomplished. Sending this list home to parents weekly is a great way to keep them informed. (See Chapter Seven for more information on parent communication.) Further, when children see the list of books read, it gives them a tremendous sense of accomplishment.

In the new read-aloud, the pace of instruction is slower and the children are given interactive opportunities to respond to questions, ask questions, and have conversations with other students. When the instruction is slowed down, the teacher has the ability to use the clipboard to collect important formative data on the children.

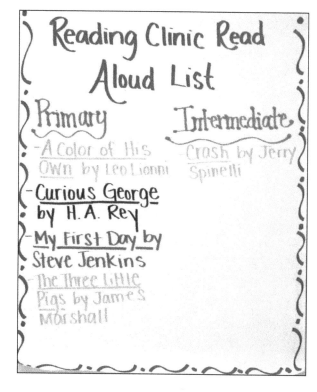

Interactive Read-Aloud Strategies

Making the read-aloud interactive with students provides an opportunity for the listener to respond and participate in creative ways, building language and classroom discourse all along. This is a perfect way for the teacher to collect formative data and information on children's responses. Barrentine (1996) discusses interactive read-alouds as the teacher posing questions during the reading that enhance meaning construction and models how one can glean meaning from the text. Moreover, Maloch and Beutel (2010) state that when children are engaged in interactive read-alouds, the discussions function as occasions for "students to be apprenticed into literacy." That is, they learn how to construct meaning from texts.

Discourse and dialogue during read-alouds also allows for scaffolding and support for students as they construct their own meaning and draw upon their own background knowledge and experiences. Balanced literacy is informed by social constructivist theory (Vygotsky, 1986) in which language plays a dominate role in the construction of knowledge. Inherent within the interactive read-aloud is the notion of language, classroom discourse, and specific talk. This talk is important before, during, and after the read-aloud. Pantaleo (2007) discusses how talk is critical to our construction of understanding and knowledge. She uses interthinking strategies to promote the interactive read-aloud. Interthinking—a strategy developed by Mercer (1995)—is using talk to think collectively and to engage with others through oral language. The language that manifests in classroom discourse plays an instrumental role in formative assessment by allowing the teacher to document and value the learning as it is formulating the construction of knowledge. This can happen before, during, and after the read-aloud.

Talk Before the Read-Aloud	Talk During the Read-Aloud	Talk After the Read-Aloud
Discuss the purpose of the lesson	Ask prediction questions	Reader response
Who knows this book?	Ask questions about finding evidence from the text	Discussion moves to the language wall
Preview the book		Talk to parents about the read-aloud
Picture walk through the book		
Talk about the author and illustrator		
Make predictions		
Discuss difficult vocabulary		

Interactive strategies that are modeled during read-alouds should also be used when children read independently.

We have had success using whiteboards and markers as an important tool in the implementation of interactive strategies. The whiteboard provides the opportunity for the teacher to pose questions and the children can respond with drawings, images, and written responses. In the photo below, the teacher was reading the book *Tops & Bottoms,* adapted and illustrated by Janet Stevens (Harcourt Brace, 1995).

Teacher Talk During the Interactive Read-Aloud

- *The teacher talks to students about answering the questions by drawing or writing on whiteboards: "You can write or draw out your responses to the questions."*

- *The teacher asks prediction questions or other questions relating to the purpose of the lesson that require the students to find evidence from the text: "What do you think will happen next?"*

- *The teacher observes the whiteboard responses and responds with statements like "I really like your predictions," "I like seeing pictures and words," and "I am starting to see a lot of correct answers."*

- *The teacher talks to students who might need help with answers and encourages the students to collaborate with each other and share their predictions: "Share your answers with the person sitting next to you," and "What could you include at the end of the sentence? Is there another word you could use here?"*

We have found that whiteboards are easy to manage when kept near the read-aloud space in a basket. Students adjust easily to the routine of picking up a whiteboard and marker before the book is read and returning it after it is over. Young children using whiteboards can have the option of drawing or writing a response to the teacher's question. In the photographs below, the students were asked what happened in the beginning, middle, and end of the story. The children drew three lines and filled in the answers.

Formative Assessment in Action: Collection, Feedback, and Self-Monitoring

Read-Alouds and Formative Collection

Using clipboards to collect formative data during read-alouds helps teachers manage and organize the formative assessment routine and process. One teacher in our clinic said it reminded her to collect the data on students as every minute in a classroom is filled with activity that calls for the teachers' attention, often overloading the demands in the moment. Teachers have great intentions of documenting the literacy behaviors, processes, and responses of their students during read-alouds but often are holding all the information in their head and hoping for time to actually put thoughts in writing. Having a clipboard with forms to collect information (see collection forms at the end of this chapter) allows the teacher to capture important data on the formation of knowledge and skills of the students, such as anecdotal information, brief observations, and other essential notes needed to make the next instructional decisions. Most importantly, the teacher has a keen sense for identifying the learning gaps as students are on a quest for the formation of knowledge and skills. For example, in the table below, Marcus "fixes" his whiteboard response during instruction as he listens to others' responses. We think this is a perfect example of the teacher documenting Marcus' self-monitoring process.

Read-Aloud/ Purpose/Formative Assessment	Marcus	Joseph	Maureen	Meridith
Read-Aloud: *Chester's Way* **Purpose:** Retell the beginning, middle, end **Formative Assessment:** Divide wipe-off boards into thirds and draw the most important thing that happened in the beginning, middle, and end of story	Marcus (9/26): Tells the beginning and puts the end for the middle but can't think of the end. He fixes it after listening to other students' ideas.	Joseph (9/26): Retold the beginning, middle, and end with words.	Maureen (9/26): Tells the beginning, middle, end, and what was important about the middle of the story.	Meridith (9/26): Tells the beginning, middle, and end but misses the important idea about how characters felt when a new kid moved into neighborhood.

Teacher Talking/Writing During Read-Aloud Formative Collection

- *The teacher talks to students while collecting written data about responses being observed: "I really like how you drew the picture. Can you label your picture?"*

- *The teacher talks to individual students while collecting written data to help adjust or "fix up" responses: "You are really close to the correct answer. Can you make another prediction?"*

- *The teacher asks follow-up questions while collecting written data to responses to check for deeper meaning: "Your answer is good. How did you think of that answer and what connections did you make to your own life?"*

- *The teacher talks about self-monitoring while collecting written data during reading and reminds students to keep track of what they don't understand: "I was really confused when the main character didn't return home. That was not at all what I predicted."*

This collected and documented information provides the basis of the feedback that is given to students. What we noticed in our clinic with teachers is that they would be eagerly writing notes during breaks so they would not forget the important behaviors just observed.

Forms to collect data during read-aloud can be teacher developed based on what skills and knowledge they deem important. We have created the following form and found it to be quite effective in practice.

On the Read-Aloud Observations form at right, the teacher noted that Michael was able to visualize using his whiteboard and was actively listening. The teacher's reflection was that the student was able to self-monitor during the read-aloud. The teacher notes Jake can recall details about characters, participated in whole group, and was able to visualize on the whiteboard. Her overall reflection from the observation was that Jake has good listening and comprehension skills.

Read-Aloud Observations

Date	Name	Observations	Reflections
7/1	Michael	-visualizing using the whiteboard -actively listening	-self-monitoring
	Jake	-recalls details about characters -participated in whole group -visualizing using the whiteboard	-excellent listening comprehension
	Jessica	-able to break down a word in context	-amazing background knowledge & inferring skills
	Natalie	-visualizing using the whiteboard (pictures and labels)	-self-monitoring -listening to key details

Read-Alouds and Formative Feedback

We propose that the read-aloud serve as an important period for teachers to provide real-time feedback to students regarding their partcipation. In our experience, teachers will give certain students a verbal comment, such as "good job," or another positive comment during the read-aloud session. This is not formative feedback that will move a student further in their learning. Rather, it is a compliment. Using interactive strategies during the read-aloud provides opportunities for the teacher to give feedback in different forms.

For example, we recently observed a first-grade teacher reading a story to the children. Her pace was slow, covering just two to three pages during the session, allowing her to go deep into the materials. The teacher broke down the thinking process by having students review and summarize what they already listened to. The purpose of the lesson was to identify the feelings of characters. This purpose was posted on a handy easel with examples of feelings that all students could view. As the teacher began to read and pose questions, she provided verbal feedback as the lesson continued. She made explicit to the children how to respond to questions, modeling how to begin a response as all the children followed. Further, she had the children

Teacher Talking/Writing During Read-Aloud Formative Feedback

- *The teacher talks to students during the read-aloud and provides guided verbal and written feedback about responses to questions: "That is a really great guess. What made you think of that?"*

- *The teacher talks to individual students and provides verbal and written feedback on how to make adjustments to the responses: "That is very close to the correct answer. Look at the title of the book and see if you can think of anything else to add."*

- *The teacher talks to students and provides verbal and written feedback by asking questions to deepen their understanding of the material: "Your response is excellent. Can you find the evidence in the text to support your response?"*

- *The teacher talks about academic language and uses examples like: "Today we are going to do comparing and contrasting of two different characters' perspectives."*

pause before responding, guiding their responses with feedback that lead to richer responses. For instance, the teacher reminded the students to think back about what the characters had gone through in the story before responding. A turn-and-talk strategy was implemented, and she guided students through the response process as well.

Using feedback in this manner allows the teacher to guide students during instruction. This means that the pace of instruction is slower and more methodical. By nature, every moment is guided as the teacher reflects and makes decisions on the next steps. In this particular class, there was a culture of feedback present that had been developed over time. The children expected the feedback during the read-aloud, were ready for it, and responded to it. This type of teaching requires a management style and routine that allows children to thrive and grow in their learning. This whole-group guided feedback allows the teacher to make sure that all the children are receiving feedback. Following up with written feedback (see feedback forms at the end of the chapter) to certain children will be important in this process.

The timing and frequency of feedback for read-alouds can happen immediately as the teacher provides verbal feedback. Written feedback provided within the same day as the read-aloud will allow the student to process the information and get ready for the next read-aloud session. We know that not all the children will be given written feedback daily as this would not be realistic. However, the teacher might decide to provide written feedback based on observations of one or two students who displayed a behavior needing the feedback. Shared talk before, during, and after the read-aloud gives the teacher much information to glean from.

Read-Alouds and Formative Self-Monitoring

One of our favorite clinic examples of self-monitoring during a read-aloud took place when the teacher was reading the book *Actual Size* by Steve Jenkins (HMH Books for Young Readers, 2011) to a group of middle-school students. The lesson began by introducing the book, and the teacher had the students do a pre-assessment exercise of what they knew about animals by asking prediction questions about the 18 animals featured in the book. For example, the teacher asked what the largest animal in the world was. After students completed the exercise, the teacher began to read the book aloud and stopped after each page for students to check their answers. The teacher moved around the room, checking answers and helping with probing questions to get the children to think and not just give answers. Some of the students responded with the following:

"What is a squid? I never heard of it."

"I didn't know that an ostrich egg was that big."

"I have a question: How many feet is a crocodile?"

These responses highlight the self-monitoring process of the students. The teacher responded to the questions and comments above with cues and probing questions, never giving students the answer. The teacher provided feedback to their self-monitoring by guiding them into new questions and information, getting them closer and closer to the correct responses. The teacher modeled self-monitoring several times during the lesson. One of the questions posed was "What is the biggest cat?" The teacher said "I was wrong. The answer is Siberian tiger, which is 11 feet long, and I thought it was a cheetah." In this instance, the teacher was making it perfectly acceptable for students to not have the correct answer. Setting up a classroom culture for risk taking is important for students. It takes some courage for children to say "I don't know," "I'm not sure," and "I didn't understand." The more the teacher models these types of metacognitive responses over and over, the easier it will be for students to feel safe in doing the same.

Self-monitoring during the read-aloud process is a critical dimension to formative assessment. Alex, a third-grade student in the reading clinic, caught our attention due to her engaged journal writing. She would write in her journal while getting out of the car in the morning. This writing would continue and carry on throughout the entire day. We were quite curious about her insights into the journaling process, so we interviewed her during a conference time to get details. During the read-aloud, we noticed that she took detailed notes about the reading and responded on her whiteboard. We asked her to tell us what she journals about. The teacher was reading *Crash* by Jerry Spinelli (Laurel Leaf, 2004), and in this particular situation, her journal entry reflected questions and responses to the story.

In the journal entry below, the student made notations with the upside-down question mark. We asked her what that meant, and she responded by telling us that during the read-aloud, she writes down ideas she doesn't understand, words that are unfamiliar, and questions she wonders about. The upside-down question marks allow her to keep track of exactly the information she was not clear on. We were

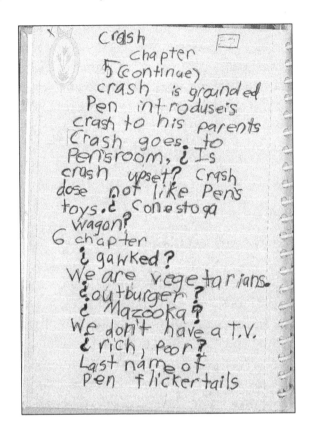

quite impressed with her level of self-monitoring done completely on her own. We encouraged her to continue this fine monitoring of her learning and told her it is what good readers do.

It is important to help students monitor their learning and provide feedback when the self-monitoring process is unfolding. For example, during another read-aloud, the teacher was reading a selection and used the word "leap." Instantly, a student raised his hand and asked, "What is leap?" The teacher stopped reading and immediately assisted the student in understanding the word. The teacher gave examples and the other children chimed in. After the read-aloud, the teacher gave the student a written feedback note (top of page 59) that acknowledged his self-monitoring and metacognition.

Nathan,

You asked an awesome question during Read Aloud. It was a great example of metacognition, thinking while you were reading.

Good readers, think while they are reading.

This is also an example of how an unanticipated response from a student forms important data to collect. We want students to feel safe by letting us know when their learning or understanding changes. Too often, students don't let us know if they don't know. Time must be spent after the read-aloud for students to reflect on the lesson. Something as easy as a "quick check" for the read-aloud can be done in just a few minutes, such as the following. There are formative assessment tools at the end of this chapter that include forms for student self-monitoring.

Date: _____

☂ Students' Quick Check for the Read-Aloud

Things I learned today:

_____

_____

Things I am not sure of:

_____

_____

Teacher Talking/Writing During Read-Aloud Formative Self-Monitoring

- *The teacher talks about keeping track of what students did not understand and might also respond in writing to students: "Remember to write in your journal words or things that you didn't understand in the read-aloud."*

- *The teacher talks about reminding students to talk to themselves as they listen to the story and ask themselves questions, such as: "Is what I am listening to making sense to me?"*

- *The teacher talks about examples of not knowing information: "I was wondering what this was all about as it is a bit unclear to me. Did anyone else find this hard to understand?"*

- *The teacher talks about going from not knowing to knowing or getting clarity about information: "Oh, now that we have read further, I think I have a better understanding of the information. Is that true for anyone else?"*

- *The teacher talks about using exit slips after the lesson: "That ending really surprised me. Did it surprise anyone else? Make sure you complete your exit slips."*

Read-Aloud Formative Assessment Tools

There are many ways to collect formative data and give feedback during read-alouds. We have developed some sample templates we believe can be used as a starting point for wherever teachers might be in the formative assessment process. We know there are many purposes for read-aloud lessons and have left that space empty for each teacher to complete. We also have left spaces for other areas teachers feel are important as well. Please note this is not an exhaustive list in nature and serves as a beginning place with much room for expansion.

A Checklist for the New Read-Aloud

What is the goal/purpose for the read-aloud?

What text will I be reading?

Where will the read-aloud take place?

What are the times for the daily read-aloud?

What interactive read-aloud strategies will I use?

How will I use shared talk before, during, and after the read-aloud?

What information will I collect on the students?

What feedback did I provide?

How did I assist students in self-monitoring?

Documenting Class Read-Alouds

Directions to the teacher: This form is for documenting the daily read-alouds. This serves as a formative assessment tool that can be shared with parents on a weekly basis to communicate all of the books that have been read.

Book Title	Author/Illustrator	Read by	Date(s)

Checklist for Read-Aloud Observations

Directions to the teacher: This checklist for read-aloud observations serves as a starting point to capture information before, during, and after the read-aloud selection. Please note that these are general observations and can be made more specific with your notations. There are blank spaces at the end to add other observations as well.

Purpose of the read-aloud lesson: _____

	Name	Name	Name	Name	Name	Name	Name	Name	Name
Participated									
Responded									
Used whiteboard									
Wrote a response									
Self-assessed									
Asked questions									
Shared with peers									
Predicted									
Found evidence									
Built argument									
Debated with peer									

Read-Aloud Collection of Data

Directions to the teacher: This form can be used to collect data before, during, and after read-aloud selections. The form has space for the name of the book, the purpose of the lesson, and the formative assessment strategy to gather information. (See 26 Formative Assessment Strategies on page 158 for a list of strategies.) Below the students' names are spaces for the formative data collection.

Read-Aloud/ Purpose/Formative Assessment	Name	Name	Name	Name
Read-Aloud: **Purpose:** **Formative Assessment:**				

Read-Aloud Observations

Directions to the teacher: This observation form is meant as a way to collect and document student information before, during, and after the read-aloud. The reflection space allows for you to think about what the students accomplished and what it means in terms of their literacy development. This form can be used for all grade levels and as a starting point for collecting student data.

Date	Name	Observations	Reflections

Read-Aloud Feedback to Students

Directions to the teacher: This feedback tool allows you to provide written feedback to students after the read-aloud. This form can be used to provide information to students that will move them further in their listening comprehension, responses, vocabulary development, and much more.

Name: _____ Date: _____

Today during the read-aloud selection, _____

_____ ,

I observed _____

_____

_____

_____

_____

_____

Read-Aloud Self-Monitoring

Name: _____ Date: _____

Directions to the student: Use form to help you self-assess and monitor your learning during the read-aloud. You do not need to fill in all the areas but rather the ones that best match today. There is also room at the end to add anything else about your learning during the read-aloud.

Today during the read-aloud, I learned about:

Book title: _____

Book author: _____ Nonfiction or fiction: _____

I know the purpose of the read-aloud was:

_____

I participated during the read-aloud by:

_____

I talked to others about the read-aloud:

_____

I asked questions about:

_____

I predicted what might happen:

_____

I learned some new words, ideas, and concepts. For example:
I can retell the story beginning, middle, and end:

_____

I did not understand this part:

_____

I still need some help with:

_____

Chapter Three: Guiding Language into Reading and Formative Assessment

Guiding Questions:

- Why is formative assessment important during guided reading?
- How can I collect formative data during guided reading lessons?
- How can I provide students with verbal and written feedback during guided reading?
- How do students self-monitor their learning during guided reading lessons?

Guiding Language into Reading and Formative Assessment: A Snapshot

Before the guiding reading lesson begins, the teacher establishes the purpose of the lesson, what text to use, and where the lesson will take place. Guided reading is part of a larger literacy routine and several activities are happening simultaneously within the classroom.

Name, date & activity	Star	Wish
Alex 6/26	Nice, smooth reading. Stops at punctuation marks.	Stop when you get to a part you don't understand.
Max 6/26	Paying very close attention to tricky words.	Use ideas from the text to help answer and think about questions.
Jessica 6/26	Thinking about the text to understand better.	Ask " Does that look right?"
Michael	Very careful reading! Takes	Use ideas from the text to help answer and think

Guided Reading Feedback

While the teacher is with the small group, other children are at language and literacy centers, perhaps working in a group. Still others might be doing independent reading and writing. All of these activities need some oversight. During this small-group guided instruction, the teacher observes and collects information on the reading behaviors of each student and could include a running record or other forms of collection (see forms at the end of the chapter). The teacher is constantly guiding, checking, and monitoring the students' understanding of the lesson. She is making deliberate decisions about each child and providing feedback during the lesson. The teacher may rotate through the centers and check on other students while the guided reading group is silently reading. During the guided reading lesson, centers, and independent reading and writing, time is set aside for students to self-monitor their learning through exit slips or other self-monitoring forms. (See forms at end of chapter.)

Setting up a Formative Assessment Routine

The literacy routine, which we identified as 110 Minutes of Daily Balanced Literacy (Policastro & McTague, 2015), outlines the balanced literacy tenets that take place during the lesson (read-alouds, guiding language into reading and small groups, language and literacy centers, and independent reading and writing). This block of time is organized around the idea that after the read-aloud, the children are either in small groups with the teacher (and these groups rotate every 20 minutes) during guided reading, at centers, or doing independent reading and writing. Within this literacy routine, formative assessment is taking place each minute of instruction. Students need to learn this routine and understand that the teacher will be collecting information, providing feedback, and helping them monitor their learning. Some of the time, it will be expected that they will be working without the teacher's immediate guidance (centers and independent reading), while other times they will be monitored closely by the teacher during small guided reading sessions. However, while the teacher is working in a guided reading session, she will certainly be observing and collecting formative assessment information on students working at centers and independently. This requires that students learn this routine and understand the purposes of all the instruction taking place. Moreover, they need to understand that their work at centers and their independent reading and writing will be formatively assessed. They will receive feedback and be expected to monitor their learning.

An example of how this formative assessment routine works is taken from our clinic. The unit in our clinic was on adventures in sports, and after the read-aloud, which covered a sports book, the children were working in small guided reading groups with the teacher. They were reading both fiction and nonfiction selections pertaining to sports heroes. The teacher continuously monitored, notated, and provided feedback of their understanding of summarization, which was the purpose of the lesson. While the teacher was working with the guided reading group, other children were working at centers on a project that required them to do research on the greatest moments in sports. They also were able to view a video of some momentous events in sports history. Yet other students were working independently on a chain-writing lesson where each student wrote a starter sentence about a sports adventure in his or her journal, then passed it along to another student who continued their story. This continued until the journal came back to its original author. The teacher was able to move about the room while the guided reading group was reading silently. This allowed the teacher to move through the centers to observe,

Teacher Talk During Guided Reading Formative Assessment

- *The teacher talks about the purpose of the guided reading lesson and allows students time to understand it by writing it down. The teacher refers to it often during the lesson: "The purpose of the lesson today is finding the main idea and we will be going over this with many examples from the story."*

- *The teacher talks to the small group: "While you are silently reading, I will be moving around the classroom to check on students working at centers and doing independent reading and writing."*

- *The teacher talks about doing a running record (see forms at the end of the chapter) or other sorts of assessments during the lesson in order to check for understanding.*

- *The teacher talks about and models self-monitoring during the lesson, using examples from his/her own life as a reader: "Sometimes when I am reading and don't know a word, I go back and look at the sentence or keep reading to see if I can figure it out."*

- *The teacher talks about keeping track of information that might not be understood during the lesson and reminds students about putting this information on an exit slip.*

notate, and provide feedback to students. The teacher was also able to observe the journal writing and follow up with feedback notes after class. As part of the guided reading session, students had time to self-monitor their learning. Students at centers and those doing independent reading had time to complete exit slips on their work during the routine.

Developing the management of this routine so children are aware of how it functions is a priority. Teachers need to make it quite clear that although they will be working without the teacher at centers and during independent reading and writing, their work will still be assessed with feedback and they are expected to monitor their learning. Managing small groups in a literacy routine is something that takes practice to work out. Students need to learn the classroom routine and practice it as well. In some classrooms, teachers have the organization and management posted so students can see exactly how the procedure works. Teachers need to position their guided reading tables in a place that gives the group a way to read without distractions. The tables also should be placed in a position where the teacher can see the rest of the children working at centers and doing independent reading and writing. A good routine is one that the children are all aware of, knowing exactly when and how to rotate from small group to small group.

Out of all the tenets of balanced literacy, guided reading is an area that we see formative assessment taking place in classrooms. We observe teachers in guided reading and small groups collecting data on students, and we see feedback happening as well. However, during this small-group instruction, teachers don't often view themselves in the formative assessment process; rather they think of themselves as teaching a guided reading lesson in which the assessment comes after the story is read.

We believe guided reading is the perfect venue for formative assessment to shine and come alive. Our new model of balanced literacy emphasizes language as a key component to instruction and therefore refers to it as guiding language into reading. Halliday's (1993) language-based theory of learning captures the idea of making meaning as a semiotic process and that the learning of language for children happens simultaneously as they learn about language and through language. The resource for making meaning is language. From this perspective, his general theory of learning is interpreted as "learning through language." Most important, intentionally learning about language to inform all literacy instruction is critical for both teachers and school leaders entering into Common Core implementation. Language takes on many different forms (Policastro & McTague, 2015). Swain (2010) explains that conversations during guided reading are centered on text and support students in "viewing texts from a more critical and reflective stance." During this time, students have the space to shape their ideas and reach new meanings. Teachers will need to provide more time for students to read and offer the appropriate scaffolding for them to understand these more challenging texts. Fountas and Pinnell (2012) believe that not only should students be reading books independently to build interest, stamina, and fluency, but they should also be able to tackle harder books so they have the opportunity to grow as more skillful readers. They contend that this processing of more challenging materials is made possible by an expert teacher's careful text selection and strong teaching—skills that take time to develop.

Selecting Texts for Guiding Language into Reading

In our clinic, we encourage teachers to use both nonfiction, or informational texts, and fiction during guided reading. We have multiple copies of authentic literature to select from. The guided reading library is one of the most essential of all multiple in-school libraries. Here the access to books becomes a critical factor in meeting the needs of all the children in the primary grades. When authentic, leveled nonfiction and fiction texts can be placed in a central location for all primary teachers, easy access and usage needs are met. Teachers then share their collections of leveled books, the range, levels, and variety of literature offered for the children, so it is an ever-expanding opportunity for capacity building school-wide. The decision of when to use nonfiction or fiction is really about setting the purpose of the lesson. If the purpose is to learn new information about the world, then nonfiction, or informational texts, would be used. If the purpose of the lesson centers on the understanding of stories, then decisions about fictional text are put into play. We believe that using informational text during this small-group instruction is vital. As Duke (2003) points out, filling classrooms with books about reptiles, oceans, families, trucks, weather, and other topics provides the opportunity to have teachers demonstrate how to obtain important information from text. Teachers, who use a thematic unit, will find informational texts can be woven into the entire balanced literacy routine.

Baer (2012) makes the case for pairing informational text with fiction. She suggests that "the connection between fiction texts and informational texts with similar topics can be powerful, as one genre can elegantly support and enhance learning from the other." This approach combines topics in history and social studies that, when read together, provide students with a narrative and informational text on the same subject. This pairing allows the student to follow the characters' journey through the informational topic and viewpoint.

Formative Assessment in Action: Collection, Feedback, and Self-Monitoring

In the clinic, we see formative collection of data going on during small-group guided reading on a daily basis. For example, during a unit on foods around the world, while in the guided reading group, the teacher introduced nonfiction books and informational selections from magazines and other print sources. Before the lesson began, the children were eagerly talking to each other, pointing to the different pictures of the foods, and sharing what they knew about each. They were skimming the pictures, charts, and maps of countries. They were intrigued with the pictures and had an interactive discussion connecting background knowledge with cultures and traditions. They asked questions and made note of words they didn't know. During the lesson, the teacher guided them into the text where they did close reading activities and shared their responses with each other. There was a continuous conversation or discourse that continued during the entire lesson. Children were totally engaged in learning this new information. After the lesson, the students did work in groups at centers and had to select and research a country and its cuisine. The discourse continued while the students were working together to gather the research needed.

Guiding Language into Reading and Formative Collection

Inherent within guided reading instruction is the formative assessment process. We see teachers collecting data and providing both verbal and written feedback to students during instruction. Indeed, it is "guided" feedback in which teachers are moving students forward in the learning process.

Teachers routinely collect data on students during guided reading and often give students verbal feedback. The collection of data can come in many different forms (see collection forms at end of the chapter), depending on the purpose of the lesson. This data guides the teacher in the next set of decisions about a student and instruction. For example, in the anecdotal observations and reflections in the following table, the teacher noticed that Alex was able to start writing an answer to a higher-level question. The teacher then reflected that the student was able to use schema and text evidence to answer the question. Important here is that the teacher was then able to provide feedback to the student, encouraging the student to continue connecting to schema to make connections and finding in evidence in the text to answer questions. Also, the teacher noted observations and reflections that Jessica was able to find her answer by looking back in the text to find evidence. The feedback that followed encouraged the use of "look back" strategies when reading, as this is what good readers do.

We recommend this information be provided to students (and parents) in real time. When information is shared with students, it allows them to monitor their own learning progress. In the anecdotal observations here, the teacher took notes on students and then reflected on the behaviors. These reflections are a good starting point for the feedback.

Anecdotal Observations: Guided Reading

Date	Name	Observation	Reflection
7/3	Alex	Able to start writing an answer to a higher-level question	Uses schema and text evidence to help answer the question
7/3	Jessica	Looked back in the text to answer a higher-level question	Uses text evidence
7/7	Michael	Reads "of" for "for" "bites" for "bits"	Uses visual information while reading
7/7	Jake	Reads with expression	Indication that he understands the material
7/7	Alex	Asks many questions, makes predictions on his own before reading	Shows self-monitoring to comprehend Shows interest

- *The teacher talks to the students while collecting written data during the guided reading lesson as they construct new meanings and understanding about the text: "I really like how you are using 'look back' strategies to find your evidence from the text."*

- *The teacher talks to individual students while collecting data to check their understanding of the text: "I can see that you are really making good progress with your word recognition. I like the way you looked at the picture in order to figure out the word."*

- *The teacher talks about the purpose of the lesson while collecting data and refers the student to the purpose often: "Remember the purpose of this lesson is to build an argument about _____ and cite evidence from the text."*

Guiding Language into Reading and Formative Feedback

During guiding language into reading, there is usually a lot of information collected on each student. How this information gets communicated to the students is important. In order for the students to self-monitor their own learning, the teacher must be active in transmitting key information to the learner. Some will be written feedback while some will be immediate feedback that the learner needs to process in real time. For example, during a guided reading lesson, as the teacher is noticing and observing behaviors, decisions need to be made in the moment about what needs to be communicated to each learner. One way to manage the feedback during small-group instruction and guiding language into reading is to provide verbal feedback that moves the entire group forward. In one fifth-grade class that we recently visited, the teacher was doing his guided reading/book club on the selection *Bud, Not Buddy* by Christopher Paul Curtis (Delacorte Books for Young Readers, 1999). The purpose of the lesson was to have the students understand the difference between direct and indirect characterization. The teacher provided examples from the book and asked students if it was direct or indirect characterization. The students responded on their whiteboards. This is a nice example of formative assessment in action where the teacher was able to, moment by moment, check students' understanding and answers and provide feedback. He was able to provide feedback to individual students by telling each to cite evidence for their responses and asking the student, "How do you know that it is direct or indirect characterization? Can you cite the evidence from the text? How would you change your answer?"

Written feedback happens as the teacher has time to reflect on the instruction and make notes worthy of documenting. This same fifth-grade teacher (from the previous example) told us that he has the students complete close reading activities during instruction. He then takes the written work home, reflects on it, and comes back the next day ready to give feedback. This teacher makes a deliberate decision to respond with written feedback. Providing feedback has many dimensions, offering several choices for teachers, such as when and how to give both verbal and written feedback before, during, and after instruction. The timing and frequency of the feedback will vary and depend on priority. We think it is important that all children receive some form of daily feedback from small guided reading instruction.

Guiding Language into Reading and Formative Self-Monitoring

At the end of each guided reading lesson, there needs to be time set aside for students to reflect on and self-monitor their learning process. This can be as simple as an exit slip that asks the students what they learned during the lesson, what they need more help with, and any other question that will help the teacher and student self-monitor. Building in time at the end of the lesson is an essential component of self-monitoring. Teachers need to make this a priority for the lesson and realize that this information will be valuable in planning the next lessons. In one first-grade class, where the group had just finished *The Story of Ruby Bridges* (Scholastic, 2010) by Robert Coles, the teacher asked the students if they thought Ruby Bridges was still alive. The students didn't know. One of the students said, "When you don't know something, you can always look it up on Google." And they did. This is a good example of self-monitoring and executing a strategy to find the needed information.

Teacher Talking/Writing During Guided Reading Formative Feedback

- *The teacher talks to the students and provides verbal and written feedback during the lesson. For example, in working on the story setting, the teacher could move the students forward with "What details can you add about the setting of the story? Your plot summary is very good. What was your favorite part? You did a good job of sequencing the events in the story. Can you draw a picture of the events on your whiteboard?"*

- *The teacher talks about responses on whiteboards: "Now that you have drawn a picture of your favorite character, can you label it and then draw a picture of your favorite part?"*

- *The teacher talks to students about the decisions they make when responding: "What made you think of that response? Can you tell me more?"*

- *The teacher talks to individual students and gives them verbal or written feedback about their specific work: "I see that you are writing a good summary of the story so far. Can you tell me how you think the story might end?"*

- *The teacher talks to the students about fine-tuning their work and provides verbal and written feedback: "What can you add to your response to show evidence from the text? You created a very clever end to the story. Now can you go back and add some information about how the character felt?"*

Teacher Talking/Writing During Guided Reading Self-Monitoring

- *The teacher talks and responds in writing about self-monitoring during the guided reading lesson, reminding students to talk to themselves and ask themselves questions about understanding: "Is what I am reading making sense to me?"*

- *The teacher talks about and responds in writing to students when they self-correct their errors: "I really like how you were able to go back when you were reading and self-correct the word because it did not make sense. This is what good readers do."*

- *The teacher talks about self-monitoring during the guided reading lesson and models what it is like as a reader: "This part of the book is hard for me, and I am not sure that I understand. I need to reread it."*

- *The teacher talks about self-monitoring and reminds the students that if they don't understand something, it is perfectly fine to let the teacher know or make sure to put the information on an exit slip.*

Exit slips provide an opportunity for the teacher to check for the students' understanding of the material. This information is then used by the teacher to reflect on how to differentiate the instruction to meet the needs of the students. Here is an example of a simple exit slip for guided reading:

Exit Slip for Guided Reading

Name: _____

During guided reading, I learned (summarize):

_____

_____

I need more help with:

_____

_____

Some students might need extra help for clarity or guidance on the directions for a lesson. Others might need one-on-one attention with an emphasis on the area that is fuzzy or with missing information. The exit slip identifies where there might be a learning gap and gives the teacher the next steps or direction to move in with the student. Here are some common learning gaps and suggested next steps for instruction.

Exit Slips and Formative Assessment

I need more help with:	Possible instructional steps:
Close reading	Students who have trouble with close reading might need to understand that text sometimes needs to be read more than one time. The teacher might model repeated readings so the children understand that good readers often reread text for understanding.
Finding evidence from text	Students who have difficulty finding evidence from text might begin with finding evidence within a picture, then moving to a short text, and gradually moving to longer texts.
Building an argument	Students who find it hard to build an argument might need to start with something that they can relate to in their own life, such as building an argument to stay up 10 extra minutes.
Debating an issue	Students who find debating an issue hard might begin with a debate that is relevant to their own life, such as whether chocolate milk should be allowed in school lunches.

The management of exit slips is extremely important in terms of finding out who needs help and in what areas. Exit slips should be read daily by the teacher with quick turnaround time. One way to collect exit slips is to have a centrally located bin, box, or folder for students to submit to each day.

Guiding Language into Reading Formative Assessment Tools

There are many skills during guiding language into reading that teachers will want to focus on to collect data, provide feedback to students, and assist students in self-monitoring their own learning. The following formative assessment forms serve as a starting point. There are many good checklists for guided reading that have been published. Our forms serve as templates to start the process. The purpose of the guided reading lesson will play an important role in deciding what information to collect.

Guiding Language into Reading Formative Collection Tools

Guiding Language into Reading Formative Feedback Tools

Guiding Language into Reading Formative Self-Monitoring Tool

A Checklist for Guiding Language into Reading

Directions to the teacher: The list below is a general checklist of literacy behaviors that you can document during guided reading lessons. Keeping this on a clipboard and using it as a reference during guided reading lessons will provide a way to capture behaviors when they occur. Please feel free to add other behaviors you think are important as well.

Student name						
Predicts						
Understands key ideas						
Makes logical inferences						
Cites specific text evidence						
Draws conclusions from the text						
Asks higher-level questions						
Summarizes key details and ideas						
Synthesizes using key details and ideas						
Rereads						
Uses new vocabulary						
Uses academic vocabulary						
Builds arguments						
Compares with other text						
Analyzes the structure of text						
Accesses point of view or purpose						

Guiding Language into Reading Anecdotal Observation

Directions to the teacher: This observation form is meant as a way to collect and document student information during guided reading lessons. The reflection space allows for you to think about what the students accomplished and what it means in terms of their literacy development. This form can be used for all grade levels and as a starting point for collecting student data.

Date	Name	Observation	Reflection

Guiding Language into Reading Collection of Data

Directions to the teacher: Use this space to document the purpose of the guided reading lesson and the formative assessment strategy. (The strategy can come from 26 Formative Assessment Strategies starting on page 158.)

Guided Reading/ Purpose/Formative Assessment	Name	Name	Name	Name
Guided Reading:				
Purpose:				
Formative Assessment:				

Guiding Language into Reading Collection of Anecdotal Data

Directions to the teacher: Use this form to make anecdotal notes during guided reading, specifically as an aid in checking comprehension. Some suggestions are offered on what to look for. Add notes on other areas of importance as dictated by your lesson.

Guided Reading Collection of Anecdotal Data

Anecdotal notes (phonological awareness, word study, decoding, fluency, comprehension — inferring, summarizing, and analyzing):

Name: _____

Name: _____

Name: _____

Name: _____

Name: _____

Checking Comprehension

Fiction (identifies characters, character perspective and voice, setting, plot, problem-solution, story structure, cause and effect; retells; visualizes; predicts; questions; summarizes):

Nonfiction (questions; predictions; facts; understanding text features, such as captions, table of contents, photos, diagrams, maps):

Name: _____

Name: _____

Name: _____

Name: _____

Name: _____

Guiding Language into Reading Quick Running Record

Directions to the teacher: As the student is reading, keep track of and monitor the different cues used, other strategies, fluency, and accuracy levels. Overall comments can be added as well.

_____ **Level/Lexile/Genre**   Name: _____

_____ **Cues Used**   Date: _____

Meaning

Structure

Visual

_____ **Other Strategies**

Metacognitive

Schema

Prediction/inference

Questioning

Visualizing

Determining importance

Synthesizing/summarizing

_____ **Fluency**

Word by word

Staccato

Phrases

Smooth

Expressive

_____ **Accuracy Levels**

Independent

Instruction

Frustration

Comments:

Weekly Group Summary Sheets for Running Records

Directions to the teacher: This form is used to keep a record of observations on students collected over a week. The column titles could be replaced with other reading behaviors depending on the needs of the children. This is a good way to see the work completed for a week of guided reading.

Names of students	Level Lexile or text type	Accuracy levels Independent Instructional Frustration	Example of running record as evidence	Fluency	Comments

Guiding Language into Reading Feedback to Students

Directions to the teacher: This feedback tool allows you to provide written feedback to students after the guided reading lesson. You can provide information to students that will move them further in their comprehension, use of strategies, fluency, and much more.

Name: _____ **Date:** _____

Today during guided reading, I observed:

_____

_____

_____

_____

_____

_____

Guiding Language into Reading Teacher Conference Tool

Directions to the teacher: This form can be used when conferencing with students during and after a guided reading lesson. This type of form is open ended with space for the teacher to point out information from the lesson and ways to get the student moving forward with a particular skill.

Information that I want to be sure to share with the student:

Name: _____ Date: _____

Information:

Feedback:

Guiding Language into Reading Self-Monitoring

Name: _____ Date: _____

Directions to the student: This form is for you to think about your guided reading lesson and respond to some points. You don't need to fill in all the areas but rather the ones that you feel are important to you today. Filling this in will allow you to keep track of your learning.

Today during guided reading...

I know the purpose of the lesson was:

_____

I read about:

_____

I talked to others about:

_____

I asked questions about:

_____

I learned some new words. For example:

_____

I predicted:

_____

I did not understand the part:

_____

I still need some help with:

_____

Chapter Four: Formative Assessment and the New Language and Literacy Centers

Guiding Questions:

- Why is formative assessment important during language and literacy center time?

- What is a language and literacy center routine?

- How do I collect formative assessment data during a language and literacy center?

- How do I provide formative feedback to students?

- How can students monitor their own learning during language and literacy centers?

- How can I use formative assessment at centers in math, art, music, and physical education?

Language and Literacy Centers and Formative Assessment: A Snapshot

Language and literacy centers are placed in the classroom environment in strategic locations that provide students with the ultimate space to work individually and with peers. Purposes and clear directions are set for the centers and identified for students to see. Teachers collect center data through observation and work completed. Students know the daily routine and rotation system. Verbal feedback is provided during center time and followed up with written feedback when appropriate. Students monitor their learning and productivity while at the centers.

Diller (2003) defines literacy centers as small areas within the classroom where students work alone or in small groups to explore literacy activities while the teacher provides small-group and guided reading instruction. Language and literacy centers are a necessary element to the balanced literacy classroom and provide ideal settings for the formative assessment process to unfold. Centers or stations can introduce a new skill, concept, or idea. Or they can be used to reteach or reinforce a skill. After students receive feedback, they can use the feedback while working at centers. Falk-Ross (2011) describes the functions of centers as "a place for practicing with reading elements, experimenting with reading strategies, activating independent monitoring and problem solving, providing extended time for reading, initiating reading response through writing, and allowing time for peer conferences." Peer conferences can be about books read and writing completed.

The formative assessment process takes on a different look during the language and literacy centers. This generally happens because students work independently or with peers. The teacher is in the classroom but working in small guided reading groups or conferencing with students. Due to the nature of this independent work, which is without the teachers' immediate feedback, the formative assessment process must be set up with a deliberate routine. A significant aspect of this routine is that students are aware of the classroom structure. Formative assessment in centers requires a sophisticated management system to be in place. We understand that this also requires a classroom management style that is multifaceted, takes time to put into practice, and evolves and develops over time. The first consideration is space. Centers require a special climate and culture within a classroom where students feel comfortable working independently and with peers on teams.

Teacher Talk and Formative Assessment During Language and Literacy Centers

- *The teacher talks about the purpose of the centers and makes a special time to introduce a new center: "The purpose of our new center will be _____."*

- *The teacher talks about what students need to accomplish while working both independently and with peers at centers: "Today, I expect the teams to finish the work on the debate about _____. Make sure you put your work in the team folder."*

- *The teacher talks about how the center work is managed and collected: "There is a folder for each team to submit their work at the center."*

- *The teacher talks about why the work at centers is important and what it should look like by providing models: "Your finished work should defend your answers with evidence from the material."*

- *The teacher talks about self-monitoring at the centers and reminds students to complete the exit slips: "Be sure to complete your exit slip and put it in the exit slip tray when you are done."*

- *The teacher talks about the fact that it is okay to ask peers for help at centers: "When you are working at centers, you can ask another student for help on something that you might be stuck on."*

- *The teacher talks about providing feedback to each other while at centers to establish the culture of feedback within the classroom: "One student says to another student, 'I really like how you created that project. How did you do that?'"*

A Classroom Routine for Centers

Setting up a routine for center work is essential as the management is critical. Thinking about the space for centers is a good place to begin. The placement of centers in areas that provide students an opportunity to work both individually and with others is important. Students should be able to have conversations and work together without distracting those that are working alone.

Establishing routines for centers is not an easy task. What we notice about center routines in balanced literacy classrooms is that if they are established in the early grades (grades K–2), the children get used to this type of structure. As they move up through the grades, centers are something that students expect as part of their learning routine. Many teachers succeed at creating great routines for their classroom centers that look easy and natural. Effective and engaging centers and routines begin with planning, creating habits, and reflective practice. Marzano and Pickering (2010) state that highly effective classrooms are the result of good planning, and even more planning is needed for small-group work. Each decision a teacher makes may seem small but leads to greater student learning as well as teacher opportunities to observe and provide feedback to students. Planning is so critical in the establishment of routines.

The plan should include space for centers and student groups as well as identify the rationale and effective pacing for each center in the literacy block. Planning can be thought of with five "W" questions and three "H" questions. The five "W" questions are for planning a language and literacy center while the three "H" questions are for formative assessment. Formative assessment strategies for collecting, providing feedback, and student monitoring can be found in this chapter and in the 26 Formative Assessment Strategies starting on page 158.

The five Ws for thinking about language and literacy centers:

1. What is your purpose?
2. Where is the center going to be?
3. Why are the students doing this?
4. Who will be in the center?
5. When and for how long will students go to the center?

The three Hs for thinking about formative assessment in language and literacy centers:

1. How will feedback be collected for formative assessment?
2. How do I provide formative feedback to students?
3. How can students monitor their own learning during language and literacy centers?

Creating habits in language and literacy centers begins with modeling. The teacher models the behaviors that the students are to have. Some centers may require repeated modeling and explanation, while others may only need one round of modeling and explanation. After the teacher models, students need to practice and review to ensure they understand. This management system for centers rotates every 30 minutes, allowing the teacher time for small guided reading groups while students are at centers and doing independent reading and writing.

Center Management

Group Name	Guided Reading	Centers	Independent Reading and Writing
Blue Group	9:00–9:30	9:30–10:00	10:00–10:30
Red Group	9:30–10:00	10:00–10:30	9:00–9:30
Yellow Group	10:00–10:30	9:00–9:30	9:30–10:00

Creating Centers from Texts

Creating centers from both informational and narrative text is a good way to have students interact with text independently and with peers. Teachers always ask us how many centers they should have in a classroom. We think it is more about the type and quality of centers than the actual number. Over the years in our clinic, we have watched teachers create "established centers" that remain up while the purpose of the center changes. For example, last summer a team came up with a "Debate Center," and the issue to be debated changed frequently while the directions stayed the same. One of the issues had students debating whether or not zoos should be allowed to take animals out of their natural habitats. The students watched a documentary, read informational text materials, and then posted their response with a "yes" or "no" with evidence. See the picture and teacher feedback below.

Center Project Activity	Center Feedback
Debate Center	You have done a great job finding evidence about zoos. Now you need to decide whether zoos should be allowed to take animals out of their natural habitat. Remember, that you will be developing an argument.

Formative Assessment in Action: Collection, Feedback, and Self-Monitoring

Centers and Formative Collection

Collecting data on students working at centers will be different from collecting data during read-alouds and guided reading. Typically, students are working with others at a center while the teacher is working with small groups or conferencing with students. We know that there will be moments when the teacher will have time to make anecdotal observations of students at centers. For example, it is possible for the teacher to get up from the small group once in a while to walk around and observe. However, the data collection will be much more driven by the work completed at each center. Therefore, it will be especially important for centers to have stated purposes, clear directions, and a place for students to place their completed work. Students will be completing self-assessment and monitoring forms. (See forms at end of chapter.) We have been in classrooms where there is no collection of data or feedback given to students. The problem is that if there is no accountability for the student at a center, chances are they will not be engaged in much learning. When students know that their work will be assessed and feedback provided, they will anticipate the work ahead and perform accordingly.

Collecting data and providing feedback to students regarding their work at centers will take on different styles depending on how your centers are created. Once again, we have created some basic templates for centers on pages 97–102. The beauty of centers is that they have unlimited possibilities for what teachers can ask students to accomplish.

Centers and Formative Feedback

Individual feedback to the student: Providing individual feedback to students during center time is essential. The 26 Formative Assessment Strategies on page 158 lists many ideas along with descriptions. Some of these formative assessment strategies are suitable for use in centers. We strongly suggest written responses so that students can reread and reflect on the feedback, but verbal feedback is also helpful. Some of the more useful strategies for individual feedback are: teacher observations, anecdotal notes, checklists, responses in student journals/notebooks, rubrics, analysis of student work, responses to a K-W-L graphic organizer, responses to learning logs, teacher feedback to reader response, teacher response to learning logs, teacher response to video/digital/audio recording, teacher response to a 3-2-1 strategy, and teacher response to close reading accounts. A key to using these strategies for individual formative assessment is to have the feedback coordinate with the purpose, thus making the feedback more focused and valuable.

Examples: Teacher Talking/ Writing Feedback During Centers

Center Project Activity	Center Feedback
Build an igloo and write an exposition paper	You did a great job building your igloo. As you write your exposition essay, be sure to use words such as "first," "next," "then," "after that," and "last."
Listening Center: presidential debate	Good thinking! You found a lot of information about many presidential debates. Now can you tell me more details about one specific presidential debate that you listened to? You might have to listen again for details.

Student-to-student feedback: Students listen to their peers and care about what they have to say, so creating methods for students to give feedback to each other is worth the time and effort. Some of the methods for individual feedback to students can be modified for student-to-student feedback. For example, two students who are doing paired reading of a text could each record their learning on their close reading accounts as center work and then respond to each other's recordings either verbally or on a sticky note.

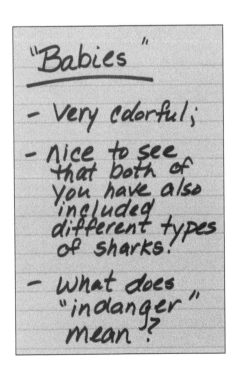

Other student-to-student feedback occurs more organically. Dialogue that one child has with another child or conversations while pairs or small groups of students are working together generate quality student-to-student feedback. Think, pair, share—a strategy from 26 Formative Assessment Strategies on page 161—produces this kind of feedback.

Team feedback from the teacher: Team feedback from a teacher is probably the least used form of feedback for centers, but team feedback can produce effective results as it reaches multiple students. Again, explanations are in the 26 Formative Assessment Strategies starting on page 158, but some that can be easily adapted for team feedback include: teacher observation or anecdotal notes, rubrics, oral presentations, analysis of work, performances, conferencing, four corners, projects, laundry day, and video/digital/audio recordings.

Centers and Formative Self-Monitoring

The teacher can't possibly document every child at every minute. Self-monitoring documentation by each student allows for the teacher to get wide-eyed glimpses of learning captured. (See forms for self-monitoring at the end of the chapter.) This is especially important during center time when the student is working with others and the teacher is working with another group. This process preserves the learning and allows for the teacher to get data that would perhaps go unnoticed otherwise. This puts important ownership into the hands of the learners and promotes responsibility for learning.

Examples: Teacher Talking/Writing Feedback to Student Self-Monitoring

Student Self-Monitoring	Teacher Feedback
I did not understand the directions at the center. I got stuck and could not finish the work.	I am really glad that you were able to monitor your learning at the center. Next time that happens, you can ask another student for help or, if I am not with a student or small group, you can always ask me.
I am not sure what to do next with my project on penguins. I have completed some of the directions.	You have covered good information so far about penguins. Your next step is to look into where penguins live.

A Center "Quick Check"

Today during center time, I learned about:

I still need to work on:

I need to ask the teacher about:

Language and Literacy Centers Formative Assessment Tools

Collecting data, providing feedback, and assisting students in self-monitoring during center time will take on different styles depending on how each teacher's centers are created. Once again, we have created some basic templates for centers. The beauty of centers is that they have unlimited possibilities for what the teacher would like to accomplish. Therefore, these forms can be tailored and built around individual center purposes.

Language and Literacy Center Checklist

Directions to the teacher: There are many behaviors that you can observe during center time. This is a list of some behaviors that we think are important. Please feel free to add others that you look for as well.

Student name						
Solves problems						
Partner reads						
Raises issues						
Cites specific evidence						
Writes to convey experience (narrative)						
Writes to explain (informative)						
Writes to persuade (argument)						
Generates discussions						
Presentation/project						
Builds argument						
Uses academic vocabulary						
Compares with other text						
Persuasion						
Social construction of knowledge and language						

Language and Literacy Center Collection of Data

Directions to the teacher: These forms can be used as a quick way to keep data collected on students organized. It is meant to be open ended and allow for your own input with data collected.

Purpose of the center:

_____

_____

Anecdotal observations: These could be observations that the teacher makes from working with small groups and periodically checking students at centers.

Name: _____

Name: _____

Name: _____

Name: _____

Name: _____

Student work completed: Make notations about the student work completed and what students accomplished at the center.

Name: _____

Name: _____

Name: _____

Name: _____

Name: _____

Language and Literacy Center Feedback to Students

Directions to the teacher: This feedback tool allows you to provide written feedback to students during and after their work at language and literacy centers. You can provide information to students that will move them further along with their center projects and activities.

Name: _____ Date: _____

Today during language and literacy center time, I observed:

_____

_____

_____

_____

_____

_____

Language and Literacy Center Teacher Conference Tool

Directions to the teacher: This form can be used when you have your conference with students regarding their work at centers. Information that you collected and feedback that you would like to provide to the student is a good place to start.

Information that I want to be sure to share with the student:

Name: _____ Date: _____

Information:

Feedback:

Language and Literacy Center Self-Monitoring

Name: _____ Date: _____

Directions to the student: This form is for you to reflect on and think about the learning that you completed during center time. You do not need to respond to all areas but rather the ones that address the work you completed.

Today during language and literacy center time:

I know the purpose of working at the center was:

_____

I worked with others on solving a problem or debating an issue (explain):

_____

List a few things that you learned today from working at the center:

_____

_____

List a few things that you might want to know more about from working at the center:

_____

_____

List anything that you didn't understand and want to follow up with:

_____

I read about:

_____

I wrote about:

_____

I talked to others about:

_____

- continued

Language and Literacy Center Self-Monitoring

Continued

I asked questions about:

_____

I did research on:

_____

I did not understand:

_____

I think that my best strengths in working at the center are:

_____

I think I need more help at the center with:

_____

Chapter Five: Formative Assessment and the New Independent Reading and Writing

---

Guiding Questions:

- How can I set up formative assessment practices during independent reading and writing?

- What data should I collect during independent reading and writing?

- What does feedback look like during independent reading and writing?

- How do I help students self-monitor their learning during independent reading and writing?

Independent Reading and Writing and Formative Assessment: A Snapshot

The classroom environment for independent reading and writing looks much like it does for center time and guided reading. The children are engaged in independent reading and writing. Some are reading books from the classroom library, where the purpose has been established. Other students are working in their journals or doing research on a topic specified within the purpose.

Teacher Talk During Independent Reading and Writing

- *The teacher talks about all of the purposes for independent reading and writing: "Today the purpose of our independent reading and writing time will be _____."*

- *The teacher talks about keeping track of books read (both fiction and nonfiction): "Make sure that you record your reading today in your Books I Have Read Notebook. You might also make a list of books that you would like to read next."*

- *The teacher talks about the importance of reading and writing as a lifelong process: "It is important to think about reading and writing as a lifelong activity. I read the newspaper every day, and I like to write papers for my classes in graduate school."*

- *The teacher talks about revision techniques and how that is what good writers do: "The revision process is something that good writers participate in, so we need to pay attention to revisions."*

- *The teacher talks about checking the work completed during independent reading and writing: "I will be having conferences with each of you to go over what you have read and written."*

- *The teacher talks about focusing on academic language and collecting information on it: "Today we are going to work on (pick one: summarizing, analyzing, building argument, finding evidence, debating), and I will be checking for understanding."*

- *The teacher talks about insights on the connections between reading and writing and collects student data on it: "Today we are going to look at the connections between reading and writing and how writers develop their craft."*

A Routine for Independent Reading and Writing

Well-managed balanced literacy classrooms have an established routine for independent reading and writing. This time for students to read and write is different from their time at language and literacy centers. However, there certainly will be time when center work will be completed independently. We like to think of independent reading and writing time as recreational reading and writing as well as students engaged in complex and rich content text. Routines set for independent reading and writing can be similar to language and literacy centers. In both, students need clear procedures, and teachers need to model, practice, and review the new habits created for independent work as well as how to reflect on the process.

Independent reading and writing requires special management for formative assessment. Independent reading is driven by a well-supplied classroom library—rich in both information and narrative texts. Independent writing is driven by many factors. Time spent reading and writing independently must be built into the classroom literacy routine.

Helping students select the right book to read independently is important. We have seen students who spend a lot time just browsing through books and never settling down with a text to read. Making students responsible for time spent reading and writing independently is central to successful classroom management. Once again, this must begin with an established purpose for the reading and writing time. Establishing a purpose for independent reading and writing is similar to purposes for language and literacy centers. Some broad general purposes for independent reading and writing are implicit but need to be stated. The implicit purposes are, first, that students need to read more because independent reading creates better readers (Allington, 2006; Routman, 2003) and, second, students need to have control of topics and authentic reasons for writing (Graves, 1994). Teachers need to think about and generate their specific purposes for students' independent reading and writing. Specific purposes could be response to reading text, finding text-specific evidence, creating arguments, and more (Neuman & Gambrell, 2013).

Motivation and choice are key steps in setting up independent reading. Choice produces motivation through self-directed interest (Allington, 2006). Self-directed interest might have students picking books that may be challenging or relatively easy. However, we also want students to read a variety of genres, especially nonfiction. And sometimes these books present difficulties for students. Reading logs or student response journals (see 26 Formative Assessment Strategies starting on page 158) are places that students can make notes about the challenging parts, and during conferences (another formative assessment strategy) the student and teacher can discuss the challenges. Teachers can guide students' selection by introducing new genres through short book talks, which are one- to two-minute pitches about the books. Other students can also give recommendations in the form of book talks. Again, an excellent classroom library offers a student more choices.

A period of time that is set aside for independent reading and writing is crucial. We suggest 20–30 minutes as an appropriate amount of time and as part of the 110 minutes of reading/literacy used in a balanced literacy classroom (Policastro & McTague, 2014). Teachers need to monitor for comprehension and check for clarity in writing. Teacher-student conferencing is one way to have teachers monitor in both areas and provide students with feedback. Self-feedback provides students with metacognitive perspective. Students can set goals, evaluate their achievement, and reflect on their learning process. Students can keep track of the learning in a learning log or journal.

Bringing parents into independent reading and writing time supports student learning as well. Parents can be made aware of the goals, processes, achievements, and concerns. Either the teacher or the student can inform the parents. We have talked about sending formative assessment home, and this can be in the form of carbon notes (so that one note is for the parents and one for the teacher). These notes can inform parents about their child's progress or lack of progress during independent work.

Formative Assessment in Action: Collection, Feedback, and Self-Monitoring

Independent Reading and Writing and Formative Collection

As discussed earlier in this chapter, many teachers wait until the end of the process and provide feedback on the product, thus missing the process and opportunities for capturing data and giving formative feedback. By being clipboard ready, teachers can capture real-time feedback and give feedback that enables students to grow and move forward in their learning. Observation and reflection is a good way to begin and an important collection strategy for independent reading and writing. Another collection strategy is the conference. Prior to the teacher-student conference, students write summaries about the chapter(s) they read and reflections about their reading in their journals. The reflections consist of three parts: 1) how the chapter reading went, 2) what strategies the student used, and 3) what challenges occurred. Then the teacher is ready to meet with students. One to three students come to the conference table during independent reading and writing time and conference. The teacher uses the clipboard to write notes about their reading and reflections. The student(s) and teacher discuss the reading while the teacher records explicit steps that the student(s) can take to overcome the challenges with the reading.

Independent Reading and Writing and Formative Feedback

When teachers do not provide feedback to students, opportunities are lost to either support and/or increase student learning. Many times, teachers wait until a product is written or a book is read to provide feedback. Giving students feedback during the process is valuable because teachers can change the direction of students' writing or reading before completion. We have observed students working independently and misreading and then comprehending a text differently from how the author might have intended. But if the teacher and student could have a quick conference initiated from formative assessment collection, then the student could experience a different understanding of the text. Feedback with one text might not seem important, but the cumulative effect over time creates sustainable growth. The student learns problem-solving behaviors, which leads to deeper understanding with not only one text but other texts as well.

Thus, teacher-to-student feedback becomes a valuable tool for growth and needs to happen in real time. Feedback that occurs in real time, is genuine, and shows the student the realistic next step or next couple of steps will empower him or her. The student is more inclined to try these small, manageable steps instead of larger, more overwhelming steps. For example, with the misreading scenario described previously, a teacher might say, "I think the text is talking about a different meaning of the word than the one you are using. Why don't you try rereading the paragraph using the clues in the text to think about a different meaning of that word? As you are reading, underline the clues the author is using to help you comprehend the concept of the word." This feedback provides the student with concrete options for correcting the course of the reading and getting back on track.

Aside from teacher-to-student feedback that can occur during independent reading and writing, students can also engage in self-feedback and/or self-talk. During independent reading and writing, students have chances to slow down the process and make time to think and reflect about their own learning. Independent reading and writing should include tools to support the feedback process.

Feedback will focus on the books and information read along with the writing completed during the independent time. It will be important to provide feedback on the number of books read, the type of books, and responses to books, such as summaries, writing about evidence, building argument, and developing debate. Feedback provided not only needs to move the student forward, but it must motivate them as well.

Examples: Teacher Talking/Writing Feedback During Independent Reading and Writing

Activity	Independent Reading/Writing Feedback
Journal entry: field trip to a bakery	I really like the way you wrote this journal entry. When you are writing, think about including detail. For example, you wrote about cookies—what details can you give about cookies?
Journal entry: stranded on an island	I am glad you took time to make revisions. Even though I still think this is a little violent, the revisions make the journal easy to read. Why did the hunters chase you?
Journal entry: visiting another planet	Your journal is full of details, but watch out for run-on sentences. To avoid them, break them up into shorter sentences.
Reading and writing research report: Al Capone	Your introduction is good. Think about how you can reel in your audience. Perhaps you can find evidence from the texts that talk about the biggest bootlegging scandal of all time.
Reading log entry	You have read a lot of different kinds of mysteries. You might try some nonfiction selections about topics that you are interested in. I know that you like butterflies, so perhaps you could read some interesting books on butterflies. Nonfiction books on true crimes might also satisfy your thirst for mystery!

Feedback notes are the perfect way to hand deliver needed information to the student. (See forms at end of the chapter.) The important point is that the student receives concrete, explicit feedback and feedback can be referenced. The teacher keeps track of the feedback provided to the student, which becomes important data. Amassing the notes permits the teacher to look back at how students are learning, detect patterns in the learning development, and foresee the need for further instruction. Over a period of time, a teacher can perceive whether students have become more metacognitive about their reading.

Collecting and providing feedback during independent reading and writing supports learning in the classroom. Teachers who facilitate student monitoring move learning from an outward interaction into an internal interaction for the student. And if parents are informed, they can support the process. The explicit information can give parents suggestions and useful guidance to aid student growth. Parents are not only informed partners but willing allies with teachers to ensure student progress.

Independent Reading and Writing and Formative Self-Monitoring

Allowing time for students to reflect on and self-monitor their own learning during independent reading and writing is essential as it helps to develop metacognitive habits of good readers and writers. Built into the routine is time for students to complete exit slips and/or forms. (See end of chapter for forms.) It is important for the students to understand the importance of keeping track of their independent learning.

The teacher will need to model for the students what is important for them to learn and reflect on. The purpose of the lesson should be an important aspect of their self-monitoring, along with a record of books they are currently reading and books they would like to read. In both reading and writing, students need to monitor their academic language and vocabulary, which includes the following: identifying main ideas and details, analyzing and interpreting information, noting author's purpose, understanding characters and plot, arguing a position, predicting the outcome, and comparing and contrasting ideas between texts.

Examples: Teacher Talking/Writing Feedback to Student Self-Monitoring

Student's Self-monitoring	Teacher Feedback
The book was too easy for me, and I finished it really fast. It was just an OK book.	Next time, let's make sure that you have a book that is more difficult and challenging. I know that you are interested in dinosaurs, and we have some books that are much more difficult than the book you read.
This book was a perfect match for me. I really like it.	I'm glad that it was a perfect match. We have more books in this series, so it might be a good idea for you to continue with this author.
This book was boring for me, and I didn't finish it.	Sometimes I don't finish a book that I start. Were there reasons that made it boring? What book would you like to select next?
I didn't like this book.	It is OK not to like every book that you read. Sometimes, I don't like the book that I selected to read. Can you give some reasons why you didn't like the book? Let's work tomorrow on finding a book that matches your interest.
The book was too hard for me, though I did like looking at the pictures about animals.	I am glad that you were able to tell me that the book was too hard but you were able to look at the pictures. I know just the right animal book for your next selection.

Independent Reading and Writing Formative Assessment Tools

As children read and write independently, it will be essential in the formative assessment process to have a system in which the teacher can collect information, provide feedback, and assist the students in monitoring their own growth. The forms here are meant to be a starting point and can be further developed to meet the needs of the students in each classroom.

A Checklist for Independent Reading and Writing

Directions to the teacher: This checklist can be used as a starting point and guide for independent reading and writing. Keeping it on a clipboard is perfect as you informally observe students or work with them individually or in conferences.

Student name				Student name			
Independent Reading				**Independent Writing**			
Reads for different purposes				Writes for different purposes			
Understands key ideas				Writes to convey experience (narrative)			
Makes logical inferences				Writes to explain (informative)			
Cites specific text evidence				Writes to persuade (argument)			
Draws conclusions from the text				Writes using evidence			
Asks higher-level questions				Writes using reasons			
Summarizes key details and ideas				Writes using multiple perspectives			
Synthesizes using key details and ideas				Conducts research • short projects • sustained projects			
Rereads text				Revises and had multiple drafts			
Uses new vocabulary				Uses appropriate (domain-specific) vocabulary			
Uses academic vocabulary				Uses academic vocabulary			
Builds an argument				Organizes for persuasion			
Compares this text to other text(s)				Writes using comparison and synthesis			
Understands point of view of author				Incorporates technology			

Independent Reading and Writing Feedback to Students

Directions to the teacher: This feedback tool allows you to provide written feedback to students during and after independent reading and writing. You can provide information to students that will move them further in their reading and writing.

Name: _____ Date: _____

Today during independent reading and writing, I observed:

_____

_____

_____

_____

_____

_____

Independent Reading and Writing
Teacher Conference Tool

Directions to the teacher: This form can be used when you have your conference with students regarding their independent reading and writing. Information that you collected and feedback that you would like to provide to the student is a good place to start.

Information that I want to be sure to share with the student:

Name: _____ Date: _____

Information:

Feedback:

Independent Reading and Writing Self-Monitoring

Name: _____ Date: _____

Directions to the student: This form is used to help you keep track of your learning during independent reading and writing time. You do not need to fill in all the areas but rather the ones that fit with what you completed.

Today during independent reading and writing time:

I worked in my writer's notebook on:

_____

The purpose of my reading/writing was:

_____

I read about some important information:

_____

I wrote about:

_____

I talked to others about:

_____

I did research on:

_____

I did not understand:

_____

Chapter Six: A Guide for School Leaders on Implementing Formative Assessment School-wide

---

Guiding Questions:

• How is formative assessment managed within a school?

• How does a school leader determine the professional development needs?

• What are the essential responsibilities for school leaders?

• How long does it take to implement formative assessment?

• Where do I begin to roll out school-wide formative assessment?

During a recent grade-level team meeting, the main topic on the agenda was to explore formative assessment documentation. One of teachers asked the question: How will formative assessment play out in writing a student's report card? This is a really great question, to which it was difficult to give a definitive response. Several questions contributed to this decision: Did feedback to the student and monitoring of his learning take place? Did the student realize how important it was for him to become metacognitive to monitor his own learning? There were many questions flowing from one comparatively simple one. We begin with this scenario in order to discuss what school leaders must face when beginning to implement school-wide formative assessment.

Essentials for School Leaders in Introducing and Managing Formative Assessment

First and foremost, the principal, as instructional leader of the school, head of literacy instruction, and overall administration leader, needs to wear many hats. The principal must convey the important virtue of trust to all those with whom he meets and negotiates. This trust must guarantee that above all motives, as instructional leader, he or she is mindful of the improvement of instruction and how it is delivered to the students of the school community. Leadership must not come down as a hatchet, but must fall gently, reasonably, and collaboratively in order to be embraced, believed, and put into practice. The leader must be fair in conduct, realizing not all faculty members immediately share these beliefs. This community is a democracy and its inherent beliefs must emerge with discernment and subsequent practice. Formative assessment is not a new practice, but it is now being hailed as a better practice. If through study and gainful knowledge, reflection, and determination the principal believes that formative assessment is the key to helping students value their own learning, then without hesitation, the initiative must be implemented throughout the curriculum. Slowly, with deep conviction, and taking the issues of teachers into account, the principal must lead on to a desired conclusion, always building on the trust of the faculty.

Implementing a new initiative, such as formative assessment, within a school community takes time and effort so that the most reluctant teacher will not dub it as "one more thing to do." Rather, this teacher with time and understanding can be brought into the fold. This teacher should also be receiving feedback, both from the principal and peers, and a richer delivery of instruction is the end product. Teachers have expressed gratitude for this opportunity to grow professionally. As an instructional leader, one must also be a teacher and model for the faculty of how formative assessment, when delivered well, will influence students and bring accolades to both student and teacher. Furthermore, a school leader needs to rely on an inner leadership team of faculty members who, through study and understanding of the initiative, can conduct mini-professional development sessions. A peer teaching peers is a desirable method of learning. The role and responsibilities of a school leader are not an easy burden, but when teachers beam with approval, students begin to relish and delight in their own learning, and parents give their cooperation and continued support of their children and their school, leaders experience profound and immense pride.

Brookhart and Moss (2013) state that when principals "immerse themselves in learning about formative assessments and how students learn, they become better instructional leaders for teachers." Formative assessment shifts the lens to the process of instruction, which includes how teachers gather information on students, how they provide feedback, and how they assist students in monitoring their learning. When school leaders make this a priority, the focus is on student learning. We have seen school leaders change their methods of providing feedback to teachers to mirror the formative assessment process. They provide teachers with real-time feedback to move them forward in their learning. One principal in our grant used a formative feedback tablet that teachers also use for the children's feedback. This feedback form has a carbon back for duplication. The principal keeps the tablet with him all the time so that when he observes a teacher, he can provide immediate feedback and also have a copy of what was written. When school leaders model the formative feedback process, a culture of school-wide feedback begins to emerge.

Promoting a School-wide Culture of Formative Assessment Feedback

In schools where formative assessment is practiced successfully, a culture develops surrounding feedback. This can happen at multiple levels and includes school leaders, teachers, and children. For school leaders, feedback needs to come in several forms. When leaders observe, evaluate, and conference with teachers, the feedback needs to be able to move the teacher forward in his or her own professional development and growth.

Culture of Feedback		
School leaders provide feedback to teachers.	Teachers provide feedback to students, other teachers, and parents.	Students provide feedback to peers.

Teachers providing feedback to students will set a classroom climate that promotes more feedback. Children expect and respond to the feedback. When teachers feel comfortable with this process, it is likely that they will provide formative feedback to one another to build school-wide assessment capacity. When students are in such a learning community, it is not unusual to see them reciprocating feedback to each other. One striking example of second graders exchanging feedback was evident when the concept of money was not understood by one youngster but made clear by his seatmate in understandable, second-grade language and demonstration.

We promote a culture of feedback in our clinic that goes public as well. For example, the work that is displayed in the hallways and in the classrooms has teacher-provided feedback for all to see. This is not negative feedback or anything that would embarrass a student, but rather enlightening information for the community that goes beyond compliments like "Good job!" Those compliments are not formative feedback.

The culture of feedback extends to the parents as well as it is a critical element of the school-wide formative assessment process. Providing feedback to parents must be developed and embraced within the learning community. We make it a daily practice to provide feedback during the drop-off and pick-up times. This feedback is often conversational in nature but provides just enough information to the parent to have real-time data. We believe feedback in written form is also important and should happen often, not just during parent-teacher conferences. (See Chapter Seven for more support on feedback to parents.)

School Leaders' Timeline for Formative Assessment

School leaders need time to begin the journey of developing and documenting formative assessment models in the school culture. The anticipated results will be ongoing collaborative capacity building within and across grade levels that focus on increasing deliberate decision-making regarding student learning and progress. Schools that strive to have a strong focus on formative assessment need to begin with a plan for implementation. One good place to begin is with the school literacy team. The formation of a school-wide literacy team should be a priority for implementation of school-wide formative assessment. Literacy teams provide a channel for faculty to communicate openly and effectively with grade-level peers. An important aspect of a literacy team is developing an infrastructure through shared decision-making, which can support meaningful and lasting change (Blachowicz, et al, 2010). Literacy teams develop shared leadership, trust, and a feeling of personal responsibility (Lieberman, 2000). They also build the democratic structures needed to sustain successful change (Booth & Rowsell, 2007). The literacy team should plan the ongoing professional development needed for formative assessment. A professional development timeline is meant to be one for which you can select topics and ideas that best match where you are as a learning community. A school that is just beginning balanced literacy and formative assessment can begin with the tenets of balanced literacy and move toward formative assessment in a progressive order. We recognize that schools are all at different points and will need to differentiate the professional development based on their needs. (See the Formative Assessment Teacher Survey at the end of this chapter for support on where to begin in assessing teachers' knowledge base regarding formative assessment practices.)

One School's Timeline of Formative Assessment

Our Lady of the Wayside School in Arlington Heights, Illinois, introduced formative assessment during the spring and summer through professional development workshops. These workshops introduced the teachers to formative assessment and the concepts of formative collection, formative feedback, and formative self-monitoring. In order to communicate with parents, they introduced formative assessment at their back-to-school night.

September

> **September Meetings**
> **(all faculty, balanced literacy team, and grade levels)**
>
> **Assessment**
>
> - What is it?
> - What is the purpose?
> - What are some different types used in our classrooms?
> - Summative assessment
> - Formative assessment

A discussion of summative assessment and how it differs from formative assessment was presented. Parents learned the "high stakes" position for summative assessments and how formative is considered "low stakes."

By October 1, the principal had outlined purposes for read-alouds and formative assessment. The principal started the process with read-alouds and later introduced other elements of formative assessment in balanced literacy instruction.

October

> **October Meetings**
> **(all faculty, balanced literacy team, and grade levels)**
>
> **Purposes for read-alouds:**
>
> - to entertain
> - to build interest
> - to inspire
> - to teach, to reteach, and to review
> - to introduce
> - to model a strategy
> - to study an author
>
> **Formative assessment strategies for read-alouds**
>
> - a journal
> - graphic organizer
> - exit slips   - continued

- draw a picture
- turn and talk
- Venn diagram
- whiteboards
- 3-2-1 strategy
- concept map
- K-W-L
- quick write

As a school leader observing the formative assessment process unfold, it was clear that the teachers were ready for the next step.

The teachers were divided into small groups and asked to do the following:

- Give a brief summary of the read-aloud you selected.
- Explain what was assessed.
- Explain what the purpose of the read-aloud was.
- Explain whether or not feedback was included.
- If feedback was included, share examples and evaluate the feedback as a group.
- If feedback was not given, explain why it wasn't and what type of feedback would have been appropriate.

During these months, teachers were videotaped during reading-alouds. This was done in an effort to share practices school-wide.

During the following month there were challenges, reflections, and finally, celebrations as teachers studied and worked to provide examples of their best formative assessment activities for their collections and feedback.

A staple of balanced literacy is guided reading, so the November faculty meeting provided many examples and discussions.

November

**November Meetings
Guided Reading and Informational Text**

- PK–5 guided reading focus: Group sharing to look at assessments, activities, and centers used while guided reading groups are meeting
- Overview of guided reading, steps to a lesson, videos of guided reading
- Study work samples of two authentic literacy activities that you have students working on at centers while you are meeting with guided reading groups
- Formative assessment "snapshot of a reader" given out at conferences and not to go home with the report cards
- 6–8 informational text: Middle-school teachers tasked with collecting samples of how they have been teaching and assessing using the informational text

While teachers were implementing the types of formative assessment highlighted in previous months, the principal turned to language walls and discourse for the December/January meetings. An obvious goal was to foster vocabulary knowledge and methods of everyday language implementation among students.

December/January

December and January Meetings and Professional Development, Introduction to Language Wall Assessments and Sharing

- Teachers share examples of how they collect data during instruction and provide feedback to students
- School-wide professional development book club: *Checking for Understanding: Formative Assessment Techniques for Your Classroom* (2014) by D. Fisher and N. Frey
- Professional development workshop: Metacognition and student self-monitoring for formative assessment

February and March Meetings (all faculty, balanced literacy team, grade level team)

During this period, much less concern and talk regarding summative assessment was taking place since formative assessment discussions and sharing took center stage. Teachers shared their own examples of metacognition with one another and how it was presented to their students.

Deprivatizing the Formative Assessment Process

- Teachers discuss the videos of peer teachers in the formative assessment process of collecting student data, providing feedback, and assisting in self-monitoring
- Teachers view the videos at home in the evenings; this is all in an effort to support capacity building and specifically deprivatizing practices

April Meetings (all faculty, balanced literacy team, grade-level team)

Amazingly at this time, teachers found examples of formative assessment practices within many of their already established assessments in benchmarking reading levels and reviewing for mastery learning.

Language and Literacy Centers

- Teachers bring samples of their center formative assessments that include how they collect data from centers, provide written feedback to students, and have students self-monitor
- Teachers bring samples of the formative assessment feedback provided to the students (including the carbon copies from the feedback tablets)

**May Meetings
(all faculty, balanced literacy team,
and grade-level team)**

Coming to the end of an exciting year, a feeling of accomplishment permeated this important meeting with formative assessment being the capstone of study and implementation. Balanced literacy took on a newer and more vibrant luster as final report card writing became easier and student achievements went up. This year was a surefire win for everyone!

Revisiting Close Reading

- With emphasis on Common Core State Standards, teachers have concentrated on close reading at all grade levels
- Teachers bring work samples of close reading and share formative assessment feedback and student self-monitoring

Report Card/Conference Alignment and Formative Assessment

This chapter began with the question of what role formative assessment would play in writing report cards. As the year of studying and implementing formative assessment played out, teachers gradually were able to see the connections between collecting formative data, providing feedback to students, and assisting students in the self-monitoring process. The question of how formative assessment would impact report card writing came up mostly during grade-level meetings. Teachers were able to share their formative assessment practices with each other, which was important to capacity building school-wide. Teachers brought in samples of how they collected data on students during read-alouds, guided reading, centers, and independent reading and writing. They brought in samples of feedback provided to students and shared how students were self-monitoring their learning. When the time came for parent/teacher conferences before formal report cards, the majority of teachers overwhelmingly cheered since the documentation they had collected and evidence of formative assessment was clearly at their fingertips and saved much time and effort with no need to duplicate. During these conferences, teachers and parents could assess a student's participation in the process and discuss the metacognition that transformed the learning or perhaps what could further be done to develop it. A closer bond was forged among parent, teacher, and student. Teachers were pleased to write report cards that raised grades and provided glowing narratives of learning progress. Overwhelmingly, formative assessment practices delivered their promises.

School Leaders' Tools for Implementing Formative Assessment

School leaders who are developing capacity school-wide with formative assessment will want to have a communication system developed for working with teachers and parents. We have developed some letters and other tools that will assist in starting the process of formative assessment school-wide.

"Snapshot of a Reader" for Parents

Directions: This template is used to provide formative feedback to parents at conferences regarding progress in guided reading.

A "snapshot" of _____ as a reader.

Currently, your child is reading at the instructional level _____ .

Some strengths are:

Goal:

Letter to Parents Introducing Formative Assessment

Dear Parents,

It is with great pleasure that I inform you that formative assessment is now becoming a regular practice in our school. You may soon be receiving special notes from your child's teacher(s) bearing feedback messages regarding your child's learning. These feedback notes are not part of the regular report card or conference but are meant to serve as intermittent reminders of student progress. Sometimes these messages might indicate how your child managed a lesson or could improve his/her own learning, and suggestions of how to do so will be offered. Hopefully, your child will respond to the message in a positive way. We ask you to help your child understand the value of this positive means of communication as it is an important part of the culture we are developing. Please don't expect feedback on a daily basis, but rather only when the teacher sees value in sending it home. Children may receive notes more frequently than parents. If you wish, you may respond to the note or file it away.

Teachers have always practiced formative assessment in order to evaluate their teaching and the students' acceptance. What a student knows and doesn't know about a concept sometimes remained in the teacher's memory or grade book. We are a best practice school, and now best practice informs us that this information is to be shared with students and parents so that performance may accelerate. Positive feedback and suggestions of how to receive more positive feedback are crucial to building self-esteem and metacognition (knowing what is known and what is not known). With the student's cooperation, what is still a mystery and what may need more review can be retaught by the teacher to assure understanding and confidence.

Practicing formative assessment in this way is a win-win situation for students, teachers, and parents. We cheer formative assessment to guide us toward better mastery of learning!

You will be hearing more about formative assessment as time goes on. Please feel free to contact me or your child's teachers for more input and be ready to receive your first note.

Most sincerely yours,

Principal

Formative Assessment Teacher Survey

Directions: This survey is intended to provide an overview about where you are as a teacher with your formative assessment practices.

What grade or subject(s) do you teach? Please check all the boxes that apply.

Grade-level Teachers

- [ ] Pre-K
- [ ] Kindergarten
- [ ] 1st grade
- [ ] 2nd grade
- [ ] 3rd grade
- [ ] 4th grade
- [ ] 5th grade
- [ ] 6th grade
- [ ] 7th grade
- [ ] 8th grade
- [ ] Split classroom
- [ ] Grades: _____

Subject-area Teachers

- [ ] Specialized services
- [ ] English/language arts
- [ ] Mathematics
- [ ] Science
- [ ] Physical education
- [ ] Art
- [ ] Music
- [ ] Social studies
- [ ] Other: _____

- continued

Formative Assessment Teacher Survey Continued

How often do you incorporate the following tenets of formative assessment into your teaching practice? *Please check the appropriate box for each item.*

Tenets of Formative Assessment	Daily	Weekly	Monthly	Few times a year	Annually	Not at this time
Formative Collection: Elicit evidence of learners' achievement						
Formative Feedback: Provide feedback that moves learning forward						
Formative Monitoring: Activate students as owners of their own learning						
Alter instruction in response to information gathered during the formative assessment process						
Differentiate instruction in response to information gathered during the formative assessment process						
Provide formative feedback to parents						

For which tenets of balanced literacy do you practice formative collection, feedback, and monitoring? *Please circle the appropriate response for each item.*

Tenets of Balanced Literacy	Collection		Feedback		Monitoring	
Interactive Read-Alouds	Yes	No	Yes	No	Yes	No
Guiding Language into Reading	Yes	No	Yes	No	Yes	No
Language and Literacy Centers	Yes	No	Yes	No	Yes	No
Independent Reading	Yes	No	Yes	No	Yes	No
Independent Writing	Yes	No	Yes	No	Yes	No

Formative Assessment Teacher Survey Continued

How often do you employ these 25 formative assessment techniques? How effective are the techniques you use? *Please check the appropriate box for frequency and effectiveness of each item.*

	Frequency						Effectiveness		
	Daily	Weekly	Monthly	Few times a year	Annually	Not at this time	Very effective	Effective	Not effective
Teacher Observation									
Teacher Checklists									
Journals/Notebooks									
Rubrics									
Written Papers									
Oral Presentations									
Class Discussion									
Analysis of Student Work									
Student Self-Assessment									
Running Records									
K-W-L (Graphic Organizers)									
Performance									
Conferencing (Individual, Small Groups)									
Portfolios									
Exit/Admit Slips									
Anecdotal Notes									
Response/Learning Logs									
Individual Whiteboards									
Four Corners									
Projects									
Think-Pair-Share									
Laundry Day									
Videos/Digital/Recordings									
Reader Response									
3-2-1 Strategy									

*This survey was developed by our IBHE grant evaluators Jana Grabarek and Dr. Leanne Kallemeyn from Loyola University for use in our partner schools.

School Leader Formative Feedback for Teachers

Directions to the school leader: This form can be used for classroom observations of teachers during the tenets of balanced literacy. This allows you to provide formative feedback to the teacher in real time.

Name: _____ **Date:** _____

Today during (circle one) read-aloud, guided reading, centers, independent reading and writing, other _____, I observed:

_____

_____

_____

_____

_____

_____

Chapter Seven: Parents and Formative Assessment: Sending Feedback Home

Guiding Questions:

- What is real-time formative feedback for students and parents?

- What strategies can be used for formative assessment with parents and students?

- How do you create a communication system for formative assessment for parents?

Parents naturally want to know how their children are progressing in school. They also want to know how they can effectively help if their child is not progressing. According to a survey conducted by the Northwest Evaluation Association (NWEA, 2012), more than 95 percent of parents want to monitor student progress in addition to being informed when concern is needed. The survey also indicated that 68 percent of parents wanted formative assessment. According to Ramaprasad (1983), formative assessment is essential for teachers and student achievement and necessary to include parents on. However, the various ways parents and teachers communicate do not always meet these goals as effectively as they could. There are some teachers who are great at giving timely periodic feedback that is understandable and usable while others provide feedback that parents don't understand, is poorly timed or infrequent, and/or offers confusing strategies for assisting children (NCTE, 2013).

Black and Wiliam (1998), through their research, found that the use of formative assessment increased achievement of low-performing students. By moving away from the traditional parent/teacher conference and creating formative assessment routines, parents and teachers can create more positive and productive encounters. Timely feedback can act as a proactive measure toward engaging the parental half of the educational partnership in early intervention measures aimed at correcting obstacles to their child's success (Black and Wiliam, 1998). If parents know prior to the conference the area of concern or intervention, they are more likely to intervene prior to the conference. Real-time feedback addresses this vulnerability so that a parent and teacher alliance and collaborative framework can be built. So what is real-time feedback for children and parents, and how does it get communicated?

What Is Real-Time Feedback for Children and Parents?

Parents want feedback that is immediate so that they can intervene to change the trajectory of their child's learning or continue a positive trend. Feedback that is delivered in a predictable manner and on a frequent basis tends to be better.

The Roosevelt "summer reading clinic" has found a useful technique that provides the feedback recommended by the NWEA survey. Teachers report to the parents when the parents pick up their children from the multiple-week Roosevelt reading clinic. Parents drive up to the school, have their children placed in their cars, and get "curbside feedback." This curbside feedback incorporates the three essential items of data collection, understandable feedback, and constant monitoring required for effective ongoing formative assessment. The feedback goes home with the parent and child as they discuss the day's experiences in the car ride home.

The routines and procedures that we have established support this curbside feedback. So how can schools and classroom teachers transfer the curbside feedback approach so that real progress can be monitored? Curbside feedback occurs when teachers collect data or information, communicate with parents, and monitor the communication process.

Collection: Teachers collect data every day. However, the information collected may not be given to parents or recorded in a form that parents understand, and the communication might be haphazard. A teacher who assembles information regularly with strategies that are clear and understandable and who has a frequent communication process will connect with parents more effectively.

Communication: The keys to effective communication are predictability, openness, and frequency. Parents who know that a child's journals, newsletters, or notes come on a certain day are ready and anticipating the communication, making it easier to communicate. Teachers who convey messages that are open, comprehensible, and action-oriented create a sense of trust and transparency. In order to accomplish this, shorter and more frequent messages are useful so that the accumulative messages over time build healthier relationships between school and home.

Monitoring: Clarity and lack of miscommunication are important for the overall relationship and communication between the teacher and parents. We, as humans, do not like to be surprised, so we monitor the weather and many other aspects of our lives. Parents monitor many parts of their children's life, such as food, activity, and learning. Parents want to have an improved monitoring system as stated in the NWEA report.

The established feedback loop for parents has been the time-honored parent/ teacher conference. This routine of report card pick up and/or conferencing at the end of grading cycles produces sparse parent-teacher interactions. This cycle has historically focused on grades as feedback (Backett, Volante & Drake, 2010). The first parent/teacher conference traditionally does not occur until a quarter to one-third of the way into the school year. This does not leave an adequate amount of time for an earlier intervention strategy, if required. Nor does it adequately prepare a parent for a potential collaborative alliance around the student's progress.

Recently, we saw a parent contacted by a teacher about her son's potential reading problem. The classroom teacher informed the parents during the conference that their son, Daniel, was having severe reading difficulty. The parents felt helpless and devastated after that meeting because their monitoring of Daniel's progress or lack of progress didn't match the teacher's data collection. The first time the parents heard of the problem was nine weeks into the school year at the traditional parent-teacher conference. The parents were surprised and angered by the information, but luckily they had a teacher who initiated real-time feedback, which changed the direction of Daniel's learning. The feedback was then predictable and occurred in frequent intervals. The steps to success began with information.

The teacher, after collecting enough information and through frequent ongoing discussions with Daniel's parents, recommended that he be seen daily for tutoring sessions. A diagnostic assessment was administered during the first tutoring session with the reading teacher and prior to the start of Daniel's tutoring sessions. Diagnostic assessments are a standard practice for reading specialists to determine the best fit for tutoring struggling readers who might need special resource support. The purpose of a diagnostic assessment is to 1) understand the current situation, 2) gather knowledge about the child's strengths and weakness, and 3) develop a plan for reading improvement. Daniel's diagnostic assessment was a means of collecting data to determine whether he was reading at, above, or below grade level.

The running record (Clay, 2000) was the instrument used for Daniel's diagnostic assessment and is the most often administered assessment tool. This is due to its ease of use and the quantity and quality of information gleaned from the diagnostic session. A running record is a very utilitarian instrument as both a diagnostic assessment as well as a formative assessment tool. Running records in a diagnostic evaluation enable a teacher to assess the child's reading level and ability to read material. Reading levels are a gradual staircase of text difficulty from kindergarten through eighth grade. Running record analysis, in addition to the reading level, enables a teacher to think through and provide data about how the child uses informational sources while reading a new or familiar text. These informational sources are prior knowledge; letter-sound association; and word, sentence, and story structure, which are also called cognitive reading cues (Clay, 1969; Goodman, 1969). Good readers use all three sources to read, and when a reading error occurs, they use one or more of the sources to self-correct.

The informational sources help "cue" the reader to ask questions, such as:

- "Does that make sense?" when attempting to match the text to their sense of meaning.
- "Does that sound right?" to monitor sentence structure.
- "Does that look right?" for visual accuracy.

The informational sources/cues and questions work together to create the process that good readers use to read. The example below illustrates the different informational sources or "cues" that good readers use while reading.

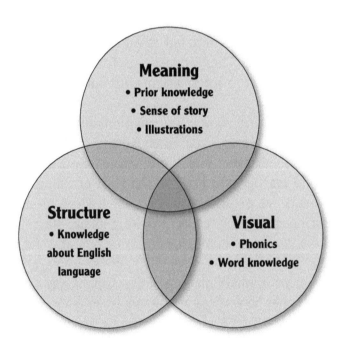

The classroom teacher and the reading specialist, by providing an informative assessment and explaining how the reading process works, empowered the parents as part of an educational alliance. The classroom teacher and the reading specialist gave the parents information as to how to support their child's learning by asking the three questions good readers ask when they are reading:

- *Does that make sense* when meaning information is neglected?
- *Does that sound right* when structural information is neglected?
- *Does that look right* when visual information is neglected?

Daniel's reading specialist confirmed the classroom teacher's original concern about a severe reading problem from his initial running records. His reading level was two years below his peers' on the staircase of text difficulty, indicating a need for tutoring and lots of support at home and in school. The data also showed that Daniel had a lot of prior knowledge about many areas and a vocabulary that was above grade level. The parents, classroom teacher, and reading specialist were able to create an instructional plan to advance Daniel's reading ability. The monitoring phase of Daniel's formative assessment involved weekly interactive feedback sessions, where the parents, reading specialist, and classroom teacher shared progress information. This progress information was then used to fine tune Daniel's instructional plan until he was able to reach his reading acquisition goals. He is currently reading and comprehending at his appropriate grade level.

The initial feedback that parents would receive, as in Daniel's case, is evidence about what level of the staircase the student is on in their reading acquisition. The data from the running records illustrate to the parents which levels are hard, easy, and instructional. Many public libraries like the one Daniel's parents visit used the same leveling system, so that finding material for home use became easy. This feedback lays the groundwork for engaging the parents in developing a collaborative tutoring plan that they can both monitor, along with the reading specialist and teacher, in ongoing feedback sessions. They are also engaged and encouraged to support the reading acquisition process through home-based activities, such as mirroring the reading specialist/teacher's instructional methods with reading, writing, and word work. The parents are thereby part of the monitoring process of the formative assessment. They can directly experience and be encouraged by their child's reading acquisition.

The data obtained by the running record can yield detailed information about the student's reading ability by having the child orally read passages that are leveled while the teacher records the frequency of reading behaviors, such as accuracy, substitutions, omissions, and self-corrections. The behaviors are then scored using a standardized method to determine which passages are easy at 95 percent accuracy, which passages are instructional at 90 percent accuracy, and which passages are hard below 90 percent accuracy. The teacher is able to determine the correct instructional reading level for the child by having him read several passages at different levels of difficulty. The running record data is collected at every session. It is then shared with the parents at the end of the session to provide them ongoing feedback. The parents can now collaboratively monitor their child's reading acquisition progress and formative assessment.

Let us look at Daniel's running record as an example of how such data might look. The teacher can take this data to provide Daniel's parents with feedback.

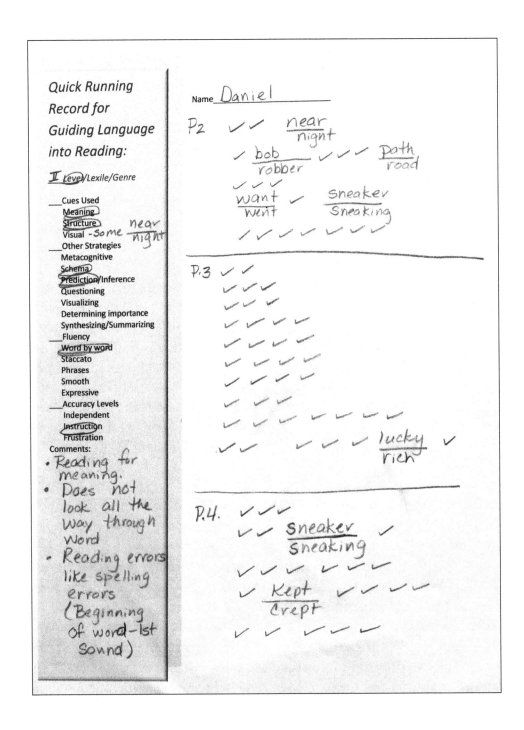

Examples and Strategies for Communicating to Parents

Daniel's formative assessment worked over time because the feedback was in real time. Real-time feedback allows parents to: 1) access information, 2) participate regularly because information is predictable and frequent, and 3) develop an alliance with teachers. Conferences, especially if they are more like curbside conferences, running records, and responses to work are all real-time feedback strategies. Additional real-time feedback strategies can be used. Below are examples of real-time feedback strategies that teachers can use. Definitions of these strategies can be found in the 26 Formative Assessment Strategies starting on page 158.

Teacher observations and anecdotal notes: Teachers take notes about a student's learning many times during the day. However, many of these notes are not written down or captured so that these snapshots of learning can be communicated to parents. We have created a simple way of taking snapshots of learning and having them go home to the parents. We have created tablets of paper with carbon copies that are brightly colored and say "Formative Feedback Goes Home." The slips allow the teacher to write the observations with the child's name and date and send it home while keeping a copy of the observation for herself. The observations could employ the following criteria:

- Explain the specific tenet, strategy, or activity that was observed.
- Define the material being used (if pertinent).
- Describe how the child was or wasn't engaged in the specific strategy or activity.
- Provide explicit directions on how to help the child at home.

The snapshots are versatile enough to be used during any of the four tenants of balanced literacy (e.g., read-alouds, guided reading, centers, and independent reading and writing). The key is to be concise and clear so that parents understand the feedback and it is not a burden to fill out.

Here are just a few examples of formative assessment that goes home to first-grade students. It is based on work during the read-aloud.

> I observed Billy engaged during the read-aloud, writing the beginning, middle, and end of a fictional story on his wipe-on/wipe-off board. Please continue to read stories with or to Billy, and have him tell you the beginning, middle, or end of the story. Go back and check the answer within the story.
>
> I observed Carla engaged during guided reading, and she was making specific inferences about Moose, the main character in the book, *Al Capone Does My Shirts* by Gennifer Choldenko. As Carla is reading her chapter book at home, have her infer both physical traits (Moose is skinny and keeps his baseball hat under his bed) and emotional traits that other characters may exhibit from the book (Piper Williams, the warden's daughter, is pretty and aggressive).
>
> I observed Jackson not engaged during literacy centers. He was supposed to silently read a nonfiction article about what the city of Chicago was like during 1935. He was also supposed to fill out the close reading account sheet and then discuss it with this partner. Please have Jackson do both activities at home and return the book and the close reading account tomorrow. The materials are in his book bag.
>
> I observed Juan engaged during independent writing. Juan's comparison and contrast of Chicago during 1935 and now illustrates that he read carefully for details with nonfiction. However, Juan does not carefully read for details with fiction stories. Please have him read fiction and ask about the details.

Here are some alternative suggestions to enhance a teacher's communication and monitoring. Some of these strategies can offer real-time feedback using more technology.

- Regular phone calls and e-mails: Use your cell phone, e-mail, and other special school social media outlets. One cautionary step is to make sure they are approved by the district and agreeable with the parents.
- Series of pictures: Take pictures on a cell phone of students' work or students working together and send to parents in an e-mail.
- A video conference: Use technology to conference face to face.
- School's online posting site: Many school districts have online methods for posting grades, attendance, and assignments. They may be able to be used in other formative feedback ways.
- Invite parents into the classroom: Many parents have not been in school since their childhood and now will see the classroom through a different perspective.
- Gallery walks of children's work: Create a showplace of work, like an art gallery. This could be for a specific project/subject area, such as art, science, social studies, etc.

Dear Parents,	The following calendar will inform you as to what we are studing in the next month as well as when things are due.					
November 2014	We will be reading the book, "Bud not Buddy" in our literacy block, learning how to write argument and studying the great depression in social studies.					
Sun	**Mon**	**Tue**	**Wed**	**Thu**	**Fri**	**Sat**
	110 minutes Literacy Block Every Day					**1**
2	3 Literacy Block – starting argument	4 Social studies unit about Depression	**5** Decide on argument topic	**6** Gather resources for argument	7*Spelling Test	**8**
9	10 Gather facts for argument	11 Veterans Day	12 Book Club- book "Bud not Buddy"	13 Science Project Due !!	14*Spelling Test	**15**
16	17 First draft of argument paper	**18** Book Club –Book "Bud not Buddy"	19 Special guest (Science)	**20** Book Club –Book "Bud not Buddy"	**21** Book Club –Book "Bud not Buddy"	**22**
23	24 Parent Conference	**25** Parent Conference	**26** Teacher institute day	27 Thanksgiving Day	**28**	**29**
30						

- Newsletters: Send home a newsletter to parents about read-aloud books, strategies being learned, writing genres, and other specific curriculum information.

- Weekly or monthly calendar: Inform parents of upcoming activities, quizzes, areas of content, etc. Above is an example of a newsletter that is sent home.

- Capstone Classroom, a division of Capstone, developed two helpful parent resource guides called *Helping Your Child Succeed in Reading: A Parent Resource Guide* by Karen Soll and Gail Saunders-Smith. One of the guides is for preschool through fifth grade and the second is a guide for grades six through eight. Each of these guides offers helpful tips for getting started and developing readers. The publications also provide grade-level support on reinforcing reading skills and strategies at home.

There are even more ways to collect student work to share.

Teacher checklists and rubrics: A checklist is a short form of the teacher's observation and can consist of a list of behaviors, strategies, attitudes, and specific skills. Teachers can use simple checklists like the following for work with comprehension strategies that are being worked on:

> **Proficient readers do the following when constructing meaning from their reading:**
>
> _____ Metacognition
>
> _____ Schema
>
> _____ Predicting and inference
>
> _____ Visualizing
>
> _____ Questioning
>
> _____ Determining importance
>
> _____ Summary and synthesizing

Teachers can make this simple checklist more complex by putting columns to the left of the list that might include information about when the strategies were introduced and progress and mastery. A column for dates could also be inserted. Teachers might also give definitions of the strategies or other information, depending on his/her parent population. Wiliam (2011) incorporates a new component into the checklist: the student records something about his or her contributions. Thus, the simple checklist can be changed to an "I-you-we" checklist.

A more detailed formative assessment is the rubric, which is a set of criteria that details the explanation of a student's learning. The predetermined criteria can be used for journals/notebooks, projects, performances, portfolios, and video/audio recordings. Rubrics can be sent home prior to embarking on the different tasks. Parents can then have a realistic view of the learning process.

Analysis of student work and student self-assessment: Fisher and Frey (2007) call this descriptive feedback with specific suggestions for meeting the criteria related to the work. The goal is to improve work through these detailed suggestions. Another similar analysis of work is the student self-assessment in which a student analyzes her work and offers herself specific feedback. The analyses could be in a notebook and go back and forth to the parent, teacher, and child, thus creating more enriched communication for improvement.

Student portfolios: Teachers and/or students collect completed student work in a portfolio, and then the teacher or student displays the work and discusses it. Portfolios are an incremental view of work because new and better work is added and old work is not discarded. The work illustrates the process of learning over time. Some schools/classrooms have special portfolio days, during which students lead discussions about their work to parents and other invited guests.

Exit/admit slips: Exit slips are an effective way to check for a student's understanding. Teachers use preprinted papers, index cards, or scratch paper and then have students write a response about a predetermined question or simply what they have learned prior to exiting the class or lesson. After the teacher has read the slips, she can record information and send the slip home. An alternative version of the classic exit slip is the exit placemat (Wiliam, 2011), which has students using paper like a placemat and recording more data about their learning. The admit slip differs in that it is used to have students write prior to their learning process or about a specific question. Teachers can have students compare their admit slips to their exit slips to see growth.

Other real-time formative feedback strategies that are sent home to parents include:

- Responses to student journals or notebooks
- Responses to oral presentations, projects, or performances
- Responses to learning logs or readings
- Responses to video/audio recordings

Many teachers require students in their classes to use response journals to strengthen comprehension through written or pictorial forms. So naturally, many teachers also encourage reading response journals at home. Soll also constructed a journal for parents to have their children use at home called *Reading Journal Response*. Per the research, children who not only respond verbally to text but also with a picture or in a written form create deeper connections to reading (Applebee, 1984; Emig, 1977; Klein, 1999; Smith, 1988; Stotsky, 1982). A productive response for journals, notebooks, and other written material is commenting on two items that were good and offering one suggestion for improvement.

Teachers create writing communities in their classroom, but parents can also create family writing groups at home. One book that can help families establish and continue home writing routines is *Writing with Families: Strengthening the Home/School Connection with Family Scribe Groups* (Maupin House, 2006) by S. Arthur Kelly. Kelly explains in a step-by-step manner how to create a family writing community.

Working with Parents to Understand Formative Learning Progress

Balance between parents and a teacher is like a dance that neither partner is leading because all parties are focused on the learning equally. To keep the focus on formative learning progress, teachers must think about the nuances of their messages and steps for developing a good communication system.

Feedback needs to clear and explicit so that parents know how to support their children's learning. Sometimes teachers give compliments about a child, such as "He did a nice job with his essay" or "He tried hard to summarize the story." These compliments are pleasant but do not communicate what parents want or need to know to be supportive and engaged in their child's education. Parents want information that is usable and understandable.

Teachers need to make sure they explain any professional terms or jargon to make their messages clear to parents. For example, parents may not know the ins and outs of what makes a text complex, but they can easily use the well-known "five-finger rule" for selecting material for their child to read independently. The five-finger rule is that if a child is reading a book and has problems with more than five words on a page, then the book is too hard. This is easy and simple for a parent to follow in helping a child select a book for independent reading.

Creating a step-by-step system is easy, but the most important aspect is getting started. Teachers can start any time, collect and dispense information, establish a communication cycle, illustrate progress, and revise the process. The process will and can look different for every teacher.

A Step-by-Step Guide for Developing a Communication System for Feedback to Parents

Step one: Get started: Getting started is probably the hardest and most important aspect in developing a system for sending feedback home. The teacher can decide to use the formative feedback slips discussed previously. The use of some type of grid to record the children who were observed, what the observation was, and when formative assessment was sent home is another idea. Strategies involving direct observations of students are a good place to begin and include:

• Anecdotal records
• Checklists
• Formative feedback slips

The classroom teacher is not limited to these suggestions and can come up with a feedback system of her own as long as it has the three essential elements of data collection, understandable feedback, and the documentation of observations that note progress over time. Try to cover as much of the class as possible as quickly as possible. Explain to parents in a newsletter and/or at a first open house what formative assessment is and how you will be communicating it so they will be anticipating and reading the formative assessment.

Step two: Give data: Begin to collect the observational data in a way that will be understandable by parents. The teacher and reading specialist in Daniel's case communicated the running record results in terms that allowed Daniel's parents to understand what was going on with their son's reading. This information was given weekly and further enabled the parents to provide support for their child's learning at home.

Step three: Create a regular communication cycle: Step three is important for creating an interactive cycle of communicating problems and progress in order to reinforce the student's literacy progress. The interactive cycle of communication requires a two-way flow of information from teacher to parents and from parents to teacher. The communication needs to be as frequent as possible without being lengthy in duration. This step can be face to face or by phone, e-mail, or other social media. It is important that the way feedback is communicated to parents across the student population of your classroom is uniform.

Step four: Show progress: Formative assessment is powerful when children are involved with their learning progress. It is even more powerful when their efforts toward improvement are concretely demonstrated. One way to illustrate ongoing progress is to compile the feedback into a cumulative summary. Displaying a student's progression can be documented and put in graphs and charts to help visualize progress. By presenting progress in a visual chart or graph, not only can the parents see the progress but so can the student. And everyone can participate in the concrete evidence of success.

Step five: Revise and reflect: The process of designing a data collection system, providing an understandable feedback system, and having ongoing monitoring of student progress is an evolutionary process. This is a process that each individual teacher needs to tailor to his or her own particular situation and classroom setting. Teachers will likely go through trial and error when developing a system that works best for their unique environment. This will probably involve individual research, evaluation, application, and revision, as well as collective discussions of ideas. Remember that there is no one way to do formative assessment with students and parents. The most important aspect is for teachers to find something that works for them while advancing the goal of creating a communication system for feedback to parents. The ultimate goal of education will be achieved, which is to advance student learning with the help and support of parents.

Teacher Tools for Communicating Formative Assessment to Parents

Teachers need tools for communicating feedback in an efficient and effective manner. The following formative assessment forms can support teachers' communication to parents. This is a brief sampling and starting point for the process. Teachers can create their own forms depending on the needs of both students and parents. The purpose of sharing formative assessment with parents is to create better communication and more productive instruction and learning for students.

Parent Letter from the Teacher about Formative Assessment

Directions to the teacher: This parent letter serves as a starting point for the communication process. Please note that this general letter can be made more specific with your observations, needs, or knowledge about the student. The main purpose is to start the process and continue it.

Dear Parents,

It is with great anticipation and pleasure that I inform you of the practice of formative assessment in my classroom. I have seen our students react with happiness as they demonstrate knowledge of a particular skill. Sometimes they realize they need to have a bit of review to really understand the concept. This is all part of formative assessment: checking up on their learning and knowledge. I am privileged to be the one to do the checking and rechecking to support your child's progress.

Soon we will share your child's progress through positive notes of accomplishment and support on how you can help your child practice skills and strategies at home. This is a win for all concerned. I can adjust my teaching to the needs of students, and they can review and relearn what they need to know. You, as parent, can be a part of this process by encouraging your child's work at home. I may write more notes to students than to parents, so I hope your child shares these with you. You may choose to respond to my notes or simply file them away in your child's memory folder. Please do not expect a note on a regular basis. I will send them as I feel they are needed.

I will provide more information about the formative assessment process when we meet during conferences. Know that this does not replace the report card or conference but instead enhances the overall assessment process.

Most sincerely yours,

Formative Assessment Goes Home

Directions to the teacher: Classroom teachers can write feedback and use this form regularly. This can be on the form or simply a slip of paper that says "Today I observed your child" with a place for the child's name, the date, and the observation.

Name: _____ **Date:** _____

Dear Parents,

Today I observed your child:

_____

_____

_____

_____

_____

_____

_____

_____

_____

_____

Admit/Exit Slips for Formative Assessment

Directions to the teacher: Prior to teaching, students are given admit/exit slips for the general function of setting up a purpose for learning or reading a text or to capture a student's knowledge after teaching. Teachers have the student complete admit slips prior to the lesson and exit slips after a lesson. The following are some general examples.

Admit Slip Prompts:

Write one or more things that you already know about _____ .

Write one question that you have about _____ .

Write about the strategies you will use to read this text.

Exit Slip Prompts:

What did you learn today?

What was difficult or confusing, and why?

What questions do you still have?

If you were going to create a question for a test, what would it be?

What were the important ideas and why?

Summarize your learning in 20 words or less.

What can your parents do to help you learn this better?

References

Afflerbach, P. (2014). Self-assessment and reading success. *Reading Today.* (32)3.

Allington, R. L. (2006). *What really matters for struggling readers: Designing research-based programs.* (2nd edition). Boston, MA: Pearson.

Andler, K. (2014). Nonfiction in the classroom: Exciting adventure or perilous journey. *Illinois Reading Council Journal.* 43(1).

Andrade, H. & Valtcheva, A. (2009). Promoting learning and achievement through self-assessment. *Theory into Practice,* 48:12–19.

Applebee, A. (1984). Writing and reasoning. *Review of Educational Research,* 54, 577–596.

Asselin, M. (1999). Balanced literacy. *Teacher Librarian,* 27(1), 69–70.

Backett, D., Volante, L. & Drake, S. (2010). Formative assessment: Bridging the research-practice divide. *Education Canada,* 50(3), 44–47.

Baer, A. (2012). Pairing books for learning: The union of informational and fiction. *The History Teacher,* 45(2).

Baker, L. & Brown, A. L. (1984). Cognitive monitoring in reading. In J. Flood (Ed.). *Understanding reading comprehension: Cognition, language, and the structure of prose.* (21–24). Newark, DE: International Reading Association.

Barrentine, S. J. (1996). Engaging with interactive read-alouds. *The Reading Teacher,* 50, 36–43.

Blachowicz, C. Z., Buhle, R., Ogle, D., Frost, S., Correa, A. & Kinner, J. (2010). Hit the ground running: Ten ideas for preparing and supporting urban literacy coaches. *The Reading Teacher,* 63(5), 348–359.

Black, P. & Wiliam, D. (1998). Assessment and classroom learning. *Assessment in Education: Principles, Policy & Practice,* 5(1), 7–73.

Bloom, B. S. (1971). *Mastery learning: Theory and practice.* New York: Hold Rinehart & Winston.

Bloom, B. S. (1976). *Human characteristics and school learning.* New York: McGraw-Hill.

Bloom, B. S. (1977). *Human characteristics and school learning.* New York: McGraw-Hill.

Booth, D. W. (2009). *Whatever happened to language arts?* Portland, ME: Stenhouse.

Booth, D. & Rowsell, J. (2007). *The literacy principal: Leading, supporting and assessing reading and writing initiatives*. Portland, ME: Stenhouse.

Boyd-Batstone, P. (2006). "Focused anecdotal records assessment (ARA): A standards based tool for authentic assessment." In (Shelby Barrentine & Sandra Stokes, eds.) *Reading assessment: Principles and practices for elementary teachers*. Newark, DE: International Reading Association.

Brookhart, S. (2008). *How to give effective feedback to your students*. Alexandria, VA: ASCD.

Brookhart, S. & Moss, M. (2013). Leading by learning. *Phi Delta Kappan*. 94(88), 13–17.

Burke, K. (1994). *How to assess authentic learning*. Palatine, IL: IRI/Skylight Publishing.

Burke, D. & Pieterick, J. (2010). *Giving students effective written feedback*. Berkshire, England: McGraw-Hill.

California Department of Education (1996). "Teaching reading: A balanced comprehensive approach to teaching reading in prekindergarten through grade three." Sacramento, CA: California Department of Education.

Chappuis, S. & Chappuis, J. (2007). The best value in formative assessment. *Educational Leadership* 65(4), 14–19.

Clay, M. M. (1969). Reading errors and self-correction behavior. *British Journal of Educational Psychology*, 39, 47–56.

Clay, M. (1993). *Reading recovery: A guidebook for teachers in training*. Portsmouth, NH: Heinemann.

Clay, M. M. (2000). *Running records: For classroom teachers*. Portsmouth, NH: Heinemann.

Cohen, V. L. & Cowen, J. E. (2011). *Literacy for children in an information age: Teaching reading, writing, and thinking* (2nd ed.). Belmont, CA: Wadsworth, Cengage Learning.

Common Core State Standards Initiative (2011). Retrieved September 15, 2014 from http://www.corestandards.org/.

Council of Chief State School Officers (CCSSO) (2008). *Attributes of effective formative assessments*. A work product coordinated and led by Sarah McMannus, North Carolina Department of Public Instruction, for the Formative Assessment for Students and Teachers (FAST) Collaborative. Washington, DC: Council of Chief State School Officers.

Cunningham, P. M. & Allington, R. L. (2007). *Classrooms that work: They all can read and write*. Upper Saddle River, NJ: Pearson.

Curtis, C. P. (1999). *Bud, Not Buddy.* New York: Delacorte Books for Young Readers.

Crooks, T. J. (1988). The impact of classroom evaluation practices on students. *Review of Educational Research,* 58, pp. 438–481.

Danielson Group (2013). *The Framework.* Retrieved January 12, 2015 from http://danielsongroup.org/framework.

Dargusch, J. (2014). Teachers as mediators: Formative practices with assessment criteria and standards. *Australian Journal of Language and Literacy,* 37(3).

Diller, D. (2003). *Literacy work stations: Making centers work.* Portland, ME: Stenhouse.

Dodge, J. (2009). *25 Quick formative assessments for a differentiated classroom.* New York: Scholastic.

Duke, N. (2003). Beyond once upon a time. *Instructor,* November/December, 23–26.

Dyer, K. (2014). 33 digital tools for advancing formative assessment in the classroom. Portland, OR. Retrieved November 2014 from https://www.nwea.org/blog/2014/33-digital-tools-advancing-formative-assessment-classroom/.

Edutopia: Schools That Work. Use formative assessment to differentiate instruction. Retrieved December 2014 from http://www.edutopia.org/stw-differentiated-instruction-learning-styles-video.

Emig, J. (1977). Writing as a mode of learning. *College Composition and Communication,* 28, 122–128.

Falk-Ross, F. (2011). Helping literacy centers come alive for teachers: Transitions into use of interactive small group reading stations. *College Reading Association Yearbook.* Issue 29, 237–247.

Fitzgerald, J. (1999). What is this thing called "balance"? *The Reading Teacher,* 53(2), 100–107.

Fisher, D. & Frey, N. (2007). *Checking for understanding: Formative assessment techniques for your classroom.* Alexandria, VA: ASCD.

Fisher, D. & Frey, N. (2008). *Content-area conversations: How to plan discussion-based lessons for diverse language learners.* Alexandria, VA: ASCD.

Fisher, D. & Frey, N. (2010). Purpose: The foundation of high quality teaching. *Principal Leadership.* October, 58–61.

Fisher, D. & Frey, N. (2014). Formative assessment: Designing and implementing a viable system. *Reading Today,* July/August, 16–17.

Flavell, J. H. (1976). Metacognitive aspects of problem-solving. In L.B. Resnick (Ed.), *The Nature of Intelligence,* 231–235. Hillsdale, NJ: Erlbaum.

Fletcher, J. (2013). Assessing rhetorically: Formative assessment. *California English.* 18(4).

Fountas, I. C. & Pinnell, G. S. (1996). *Guided reading: Good first teaching for all children.* Portsmouth, NH: Heinemann.

Fountas, I. C. & Pinnell, G. S. (2012). Guided reading: The romance and the reality. *The Reading Teacher,* 66(4), 268.

Frey, B. B., Lee, S. W., Tollefson, N., Pass, L. & Massengill, D. (2005). Balanced literacy in an urban school district. *Journal of Educational Research,* 98(5), 272–280.

Gee, J. (2001). Reading as situated language: A sociocognitive perspective. *Journal of Adolescent & Adult Literacy,* 44(8), 714.

Gillespie, C. S., Ford, K. L., Gillespie, R. D. & Leavel, A. G. (1996). Portfolio assessment: Some questions, some answers, some recommendations. *Journal of Adolescent and Adult Literacy,* 39(6), 480–491.

Goodman, K. S. (1969). Analysis of oral reading miscue: Applied psycholinguistics. *Reading Research Quarterly,* 5, 9–30.

Graves, D. (1994). *A fresh look at writing.* Portsmouth, NH: Heinemann.

Greenstein, L. (2010). *What teachers really need to know about formative assessment.* Alexandria, VA: ASCD.

Halliday, M. A. K. (1993). Towards a language-based theory of learning. *Linguistics and Education,* 5, 93–116.

Hattie, J. & Timperley, H. (2007). The power of feedback. *Review of Educational Research,* 77(1), 81–112.

Heritage, M. (2011). Formative assessment: An enabler of learning. *Better: Evidence-based Education,* Spring, 8–19.

Himmele, P. & Himmele, W. (2011). *Total participation techniques: Making every student an active learner.* Alexandria, VA: ASCD.

Honig, B. (1996). *Teaching our children to read: The role of skills in a comprehensive reading program.* Thousand Oaks, CA: Corwin Press.

Hudesman, J., Crosby, S., Flugman, B., Isaac, S., Everson, H. & Clay, D. (2013). Using formative assessment and metacognition to improve student achievement. *Journal of Developmental Education,* 37.

Illinois State Board of Education (ISBE). A sampling of types of formative assessment. Retrieved, November 12, 2014 from www.isbe.net/common_core/pdf/da-form-asmt-chart.pdf.

Jenkins, S. (2011). *Actual Size.* New York: HMH Books for Young Readers.

Keeley, P. (2013). Is it a rock? Continuous formative assessment. *Science and Children,* 34–37.

Kelly, S. A. (2006). *Writing with families: Strengthening the home/school connection with family scribe groups.* Gainesville, FL: Maupin House.

Klein, P. (1999). Reopening inquiry into cognitive processes in writing-to-learn. *Educational Psychology Review,* 11, 203–270.

Lieberman, A. (2000). Learning Communities: Shaping the future of teacher development. *Journal of Teacher Education,* 51, 221–227.

Lin, J. W. & Lai, Y. C. (2013). Harnessing collaborative annotations on online formative assessments. *Educational Technology & Sociology,* 16(1), 263–274.

Madda, C. L., Griffo, V. B., Pearson, P. D. & Raphael, T. E. (2007). Balance in comprehensive literacy instruction. L. M. Marrow & L. Gambrell (Eds.), *Best practices in literacy instruction,* 4th ed., 37–67. New York: Guilford Press.

Maloch, B. & Beutel, D. D. (2010). "Big loud voice. You have important things to say": The nature of student initiations during one teacher's interactive read-alouds. *Journal of Classroom Instruction.* 45(2).

Manning, B. H. & Payne, B. D. (1996). *Self-talk for teachers and students: Metacognitive strategies for personal and classroom use.* Boston: Allyn & Bacon.

Marcell, B. (2007). Traffic light reading: fostering the independent usage of comprehension strategies with informational text. *The Reading Teacher,* 60(8), 778–781

Marzano, R. & Pickering, D. (2010). *Building academic vocabulary.* Alexandria, VA: ASCD.

Mercer, N. (1995). *The guided construction of knowledge: Talk amongst teachers and learners.* Clevedon, UK: Multilingual Matters, Ltd.

National Council of Teachers of English (NCTE) (2013). Formative assessment that truly informs instruction. A statement on an educational issue approved by the NCTE Board of Directors of the NCTE Executive Committee. Urbana, IL. Retrieved December 2014 from http://www.ncte.org/library/NCTEFiles/Resources/Positions/formative-assessment_single.pdf.

Neuman, S. & Gambrell, L. (2013). *Quality reading instruction in the age of common core standards.* Newark, DE: International Reading Association.

Northwest Evaluation Association (NWEA) (2012). For every child, multiple measures: What parents and educators want from K–12 assessments. Portland, OR. Retrieved November 2014 from https://www.nwea.org/resources/every-child-multiple-measures-parents-educators-want-k-12-assessments/.

O'Day, J., Goertz, M. E. & Floden, R. E. (1995). Building capacity for education reform. *CPRE Policy Briefs.*

Panadero, E. & Alonso-Tapia, J. (2013). Self-assessment: theoretical and practical connotations. When it happens, how it is acquired and what to do to develop it in our students. *Electronic Journal of Research in Educational Psychology,* 11(2), 551–576.

Pantaleo, S. (2007). Interthinking: young children using language to think collectively during interactive read-alouds. *Early Childhood Education Journal*, Vol. 34, No. 6.

Pearson, P. D. (2002). American reading instruction since 1967. In N.B. smith, *American Reading Instruction* (Special ed., 419–486). Newark, DE: International Reading Association.

Phillips, V. & Wong, C. (2010). Tying together the common core of standards, instruction, and assessments. *Phi Delta Kappan,* 91(5), 37–42.

Policastro, M. M. (1993). Assessing and developing metacognitive attributes in college students with learning disabilities. S.A. Vogel & P. B. Adelman (Eds.), *Success for College Students with Learning Disabilities,* 151–176. New York: Springer-Verlag.

Policastro, M. M. & McTague, B. (2015). *The new balanced literacy school: Implementing Common Core.* North Mankato, MN: Maupin House by Capstone Professional.

Popham, W. J. (2008). *Transformative assessment.* Alexandria, VA: ASCD.

Purkey, W. W. (2002). *What students say to themselves: Internal dialogue and school success.* Thousand Oaks, CA: Corwin Press.

Ramaprasad, A. (1983). On the definition of feedback. *Behavioral Science*, 28(1), 4–13.

Roskos, K. & Neuman, S. B. (2012). Formative assessment: Simply, no additives. *Reading Teacher,* 65(8), 534–538.

Routman, R. (2003). *Reading essentials: The specifics you need to teach reading well.* Portsmouth, NH: Heinemann.

Ruddell, R. B., Ruddell, M. R. & Singer, H. (Eds.) (1994). *Theoretical models and processes of reading.* (4th Ed). Newark, DE: International Reading Association.

Ruddell, R. B. & Unrau, N. J. (2004). Reading as a motivated meaning-constructed process: The reader, the text and the teacher. In *Theoretical models and processes of reading* (5th ed. 1462–1521), (Eds.) R. J. Ruddell and N.J. Unrau. Newark, DE: International Reading Association.

Sadler, D. R. (1989). Formative assessment and the design of instructional systems. *Instructional Science,* 18, 191–209.

Sadler, D. R. (1998). Formative assessment: Revisiting the territory. *Assessment in Education.* March, 5(1), 77–85.

Santoro, L. E., Chard, D. J., Howard, L. & Baker, S. (2008). Making the very most of classroom read-alouds to promote comprehension and vocabulary. *The Reading Teacher*, 61(15), 396–408.

Scriven, M. (1967). The methodology of evaluation. *AERA Monograph Series on Evaluation,* I, 39–83.

Shanahan, T. (2013, October 17). Common visions, common goals: Preparing schools, colleges and universities for the new standards and assessments. *Common Visions, Common Goals.* Lecture conducted from Bone Student Center, Center for the Study of Education Policy, Illinois State University, Normal, IL.

Shanahan, T. (2014). How and how not to prepare students for the new tests. *The Reading Teacher.* (68)3.

Shepard, L. A., Hammerness, K., Darling-Hammond, L., Rust, F. (2005). Assessment. In L. Darling-Hammond & J. Bransford (Eds.), *Preparing teachers for a changing world: What teachers should learn and be able to do.* San Francisco, CA: Jossey-Bass.

Smith, C. (1988). Does it help to write about your reading? *Journal of Reading*, 31, 276–277.

Smith, F. (2004). *Understanding reading: A psycholinguistic analysis of reading and learning to read.* Hillsdale, NJ: Erlbaum.

Spencer, T. (2001). Improving achievement through self-talk. *Educational Leadership,* 4(6).

Spiegel, D. (1998). Silver bullets, babies, and bath water: Literature response groups in a balanced literacy program. *Reading Teacher,* 52(2), 114.

Stevens, J. (1995). *Tops & bottoms.* New York: Harcourt Brace.

Stotsky, S. (1982). The role of writing in developmental reading. *Journal of Reading,* 31, 320–340.

Swain, C. (2010). "It looked like one thing but when we went in more depth, it turned out to be completely different." Reflecting on the discourse of guided reading and its role in fostering critical responses to magazines. *Literacy.* 44(3).

Tompkins, G. (2007). *Language arts: Patterns of practice seventh edition.* Columbus, OH: Pearson.

Tompkins, G. E. (2010, 2013). *Literacy for the 21st century: A balanced approach* (5th ed.). Boston, MA: Allyn & Bacon.

Tracey, D. H. & Morrow, L. M. (2006). *Lenses on reading: An introduction to theories and models.* New York: Guilford Press.

Using formative assessment to differentiate instruction. Retrieved November 2014 from http://www.edutopia.org/stw-differentiated-instruction-learning-styles-video

Vygotsky, L. (1978). *Mind in society: The development of higher psychological processes.* Cambridge, MA: Harvard University Press.

Vygotsky, L. (1986). *Thought and language.* Cambridge, MA: MIT Press.

Wang, M. C. & Palinscar, A. S. (1989). Teaching students to assume an active role in their learning. In M. C. Reynolds (Ed.), *Knowledge base for the beginning teacher.* Elmsford, NY: Pergamon.

Welcome To Achieve | Achieve. (n.d.). *Welcome To Achieve | Achieve.* Retrieved August 20, 2014 from http://achieve.org/.

Wells, R. (1997). *Bunny cakes.* New York: Penguin.

Wiggins, G. (2012). Seven keys to effective feedback. *Educational Leadership,* Number 1, (10–16).

Wiliam, D. (2011). *Embedded formative assessment.* Bloomington, IN: Solution Tree Press.

Yopp, R. H. & Yopp, H. K. (2006). Informational text as read-alouds at school and home. *Journal of Literacy Research,* 38(1), 37–51.

26 Formative Assessment Strategies

1. **Anecdotal notes:** An authentic form of formative assessment in which the teacher actively records the student's behaviors, use of strategies, and/or other noteworthy information that could be useful for the student's learning or the teacher's instruction (Boyd-Batstone, 2006). Pages 43, 93

2. **Analysis of student work:** This form is sometimes called descriptive feedback. It can be either oral or written. The feedback is learner specific and should be about specific criteria related to the work with suggestions for improvement. (Fisher & Frey, 2007) Pages 93, 142

3. **Class discussion:** This is the sharing of thoughts and ideas about a topic in either a whole-class or small-group setting. Students explore knowledge through the give and take of questions, probes, reflections, responses, and interactions. Teachers can record students' interactions by using anecdotal notes, video clips, checklists, or other means, so that feedback can be given to individuals or groups of students. (Black & Wiliam, 1998) Pages 24, 40, 143

4. **Conferencing (individual, small group):** This is a teacher-initiated constructive conversation with an individual student or a group of students about their intentions, process, or product(s). The purpose is to help both teacher and student achieve a better understanding of the work as well as to plan next steps for improvement. (NCTE Position Paper, 2013) Pages 26, 40, 44, 58, 94

5. **Exit/admit slips:** Exit slips capture what the student has learned, wants to know, or is unsure about. These slips are handed out during class and are filled out during the final minutes of instruction. Exit slips allow teachers to monitor where students are at and can be used to give feedback. (NCTE Position Paper, 2013) Students use admit slips to write prior to the learning process or about a specific question. Students may compare their admit slips to their exit slips to see growth. Pages 59, 76, 77, 110, 121, 143

6. **Four corners:** Corners in the classroom are labeled *strongly agree*, *agree*, *disagree*, and *strongly disagree*. The teacher presents a controversial statement and then has the students go to the corner that best fits their opinion. Students then pair up to discuss their opinions. The teacher circulates, records comments, and gives feedback to each group about their arguments. This strategy can also lead to a whole-group discussion in which opinions are defended and/or students can return to their desks to write about their opinions. Teachers can give additional feedback about students' written arguments gleaned from either small-group or large-group discussion. (ISBE, 2014) Page 94

7. **Individual whiteboards:** These are simple, small whiteboards that a student can use to write or draw on with a marker, which can be wiped off so the board can be used again. These boards can be written on prior to, during, or after instruction so that students can be more engaged as well as be held accountable for learning. Teachers can see what students have written and/or drawn, which allows the teacher to record the responses and use them for formative assessment. (Dodge, 2009) Pages 45, 51, 52

8. **Journals/notebooks:** Journals, notebooks, or learning logs are common means of recording learning. Engineers, scientists, writers, artists, and students use these to record learning, reflections, and processes. Journals and notebooks enable students to create goals, make connections, and reflect on their own learning. By reading student journals, teachers can give students formative feedback to improve learning. (Black & Wiliam, 1998) Page 105

9. **K-W-L charts (graphic organizers):** K-W-L charts are used during instruction so students can document what they *know*, what they *wonder*, and what they *learned*. They are typically organized into three columns with each letter (K-W-L) at the top. (Tompkins, 2013) Page 93

10. **Laundry day:** This strategy enables students to self-assess their own work and give feedback to themselves about how to improve. Previous class work can also be used as criteria or current products. Initially, the student determines from one of four groups how his/her work is. The four groups are: *stormy* (feel they are drowning in information), *cloudy* (understand basics but missing some key parts), *partly sunny* (fairly confident, just some missing details), and *clear and sunny* (sure of success, looking for enrichment). After students have determined which category their work is in, they create an action plan to improve their work. (ISBE, 2014) Page 94

11. **Oral presentations:** One classic form of oral discourse is a presentation of information. Oral presentations sometimes consist of one student or a group of students explaining their understanding of new information. Styles of presentations can range and include multimedia, modeling, demonstrations, and speeches. Students can benefit from the teacher's oral and/or written feedback to the student or group presentation but also from the content offered. (Booth, 2009; Tompkins, 2007) Pages 94, 143

12. **Performance through the arts:** The learner creates an artistic piece and/or show that illustrates what he/she knows or has learned about given areas of study. Sometimes this area of formative assessment is also called demonstration of learning and typically comes at the end of a period of research or study on a topic. The teacher gives oral and/or written feedback to the student. (Fisher & Frey, 2007) Pages 94, 142

13. **Portfolios:** Student portfolios are similar to an artist portfolio. An assortment of completed work collected by a student is gathered by the teacher and/or student over time. The collection of work can be in one subject area or over multiple disciplines. Feedback about the collection of work can be given to a student at multiple levels. One level is student self-feedback, the second is peer-to-peer feedback, the third is teacher feedback, and the fourth is parent feedback. Students, teachers, and parents at all levels are asked to reflect and give critical feedback so that new insights and understanding about learning can be gained. One important aspect of portfolios is enabling the student, teacher, and parent to see growth over time. (Gillespie, Ford, Gillespie & Leavel, 1996) Pages 44, 142, 143

14. **Projects (see Performance Through the Arts):** The learner demonstrates understanding of knowledge as determined through a set of criteria. Usually the project is presented to a group of students or to the whole class, and then the teacher gives oral or written feedback. (ISBE, 2014) Pages 94, 142

15. **Reader response:** This is a written reaction to a text—whether it was a read-aloud, heard via an audio recording, or read independently. The student's responses create a way to document learning over time as well as to gain insight on comprehension of a specific text. The student can reflect on a single response or responses over a period of time. (Burke & Pieterick, 2010) Page 143

16. **Response/learning logs:** Learning logs and journals are notebooks students use to write daily reflections about their learning. These reflections about their learning can help students evaluate, analyze, and reflect on the lesson or help process the instructions. (Black & Wiliam, 1998) Page 143

17. **Rubrics:** A rubric is a set of criteria that details the explanation of a student's learning. The criteria for the rubric are predetermined by the teacher, and students use the standards to plan, revise, and/or evaluate their learning. Teachers can give students very specific and detailed written feedback using the specific criteria from the rubric. (Brookhart, 2008) Page 142

18. **Running records:** Teachers record a student's oral reading of new or familiar text through coded notation. After recording the oral reading, a teacher scores and analyzes the errors. Scoring of the running record enables a teacher to determine if the reading of the text was independent, instructional, or frustrating. Error analysis helps the teacher conclude how the reader used different cues, such as meaning, structure, or visual. Teachers can share this information with students and parents. (Clay, 1993) Pages 43, 135, 137, 138

19. **Student self-assessment:** Students evaluate their own work by assessing their own progress. The process usually includes long-term and short-term goals, a plan to achieve the goals, and why goals have or have not been attained. This assessment is important for student self-monitoring. (NCTE Position Paper, 2013) Pages 30, 39, 142

20. **Teacher checklists:** A checklist is a short form of the teacher's observations. Checklists consist of a list of behaviors, strategies, attitudes, and specific skills, which teachers can monitor and give feedback on at different intervals (initial, continuous, or mastery) of the work or process. This quick and easy form of formative assessment can be used with individual students or groups of students (Burke, 1994). Wiliam (2011) calls these "I-you-we checklists" because this form of assessment should be interactive and useful for student learning. (Burke, 1994; Wiliam, 2011) Pages 30, 142

21. **Teacher observations:** Fundamental to formative assessment is watching and recording student behavior and language. Sometimes this formative assessment is also known as kid watching. It enables teachers to determine students' strengths and weaknesses so that better instruction can be planned. Other names for this form of assessment are anecdotal notes, anecdotal cards, labels, and sticky notes. Each of these derives its name from what observations are recorded on. The critical point is selecting an organization style that fits one's needs, recording the students' behaviors over time, and reflecting and sharing these reflections with students for improved learning and teaching. (NCTE Position Paper, 2013) Page 139

22. **Think-pair-share:** The teacher presents a question (higher level, standard targeted). Students have 20–30 seconds to think on their own. On a signal, the students turn to a partner and discuss their thoughts for about one minute, then they share with the class. During the discussions, teachers eavesdrop on a few of the conversations, thus enabling the teacher to collect evidence from a student and/or group and then give the student or group formative assessment. (ISBE, 2014) Page 94

23. **Thumbs-up and thumbs-down:** This formative assessment allows instruction to continue without distractions from the lesson but enables a teacher to check quickly for understanding. For example, students who understand or agree show a thumbs-up, students who do not understand or who disagree show a thumbs-down, students who are confused move their thumbs back and forth over their heads, and students who cannot hear place a hand behind their ear. (Himmele & Himmele, 2011).

24. **Turn and talk:** During this formative assessment, students are prompted to turn to a student next to them and discuss a question or their ideas for a set amount of time. The discussion depends on the purpose that teacher has determined. As the students are talking, teacher(s) can listen in on the discussion to collect data and then provide written or verbal feedback to individual students or groups. (Himmele & Himmele, 2011). Page 46

25. **Videos/audio recordings:** A visual or audio recording of a student's reading, performance, or project enables a student to reflect on the work. This is an effective way to provide self-feedback. (Edutopia, 2014). Page 94

26. **3-2-1 strategy:** This formative assessment is similar to an exit slip, except it has specific criteria. The criteria are that a student writes three (3) things he/she learned today, two (2) things he/she found interesting, and one (1) question that he/she still has. Hence the term "3-2-1 strategy." This form of formative assessment gives the teacher feedback about the student's learning. (Dodge, 2009) Page 93

110 Minutes of Formative Assessment Strategies

Directions to the teacher: We have created a list of formative assessment strategies from the current literature. We have listed them here so you can get a sense of where they might fit into your balanced literacy instruction.

26 Formative Assessment Strategies	Read-Alouds	Guided reading/ book club	Centers	Independent reading and writing
Anecdotal notes				
Analysis of student work				
Class discussion				
Conferencing (individual, small groups)				
Exit/admit slips				
Four corners				
Individual whiteboards				
Journals/notebooks				
K-W-L charts				
Laundry day				
Oral presentations				
Performance through the arts				
Portfolios				
Projects				
Reader response				
Response/learning logs				
Rubrics				
Running records				
Student self-assessment				
Teacher checklists				
Teacher observations				
Think-pair-share				
Thumbs-up and thumbs-down				
Turn and talk				
Videos/audio recordings				
3-2-1 strategy				

Notes

Notes

Notes

Notes

Maupin House *by*
capstone
professional

At Maupin House by Capstone Professional, we continue to look for professional development resources that support grades K–8 classroom teachers in areas, such as these:

Literacy	**Language Arts**
Content-Area Literacy	**Research-Based Practices**
Assessment	**Inquiry**
Technology	**Differentiation**
Standards-Based Instruction	**School Safety**
Classroom Management	**School Community**

If you have an idea for a professional development resource, visit our Become an Author website at:

http://maupinhouse.com/index.php/become-an-author

There are two ways to submit questions and proposals.

1. You may send them electronically to:

http://maupinhouse.com/index.php/become-an-author

2. You may send them via postal mail. Please be sure to include a self-addressed stamped envelope for us to return materials.

Acquisitions Editor
Capstone Professional
1 N. LaSalle Street, Suite 1800
Chicago, IL 60602